The Quiet Icon

The Influential Life of Robert E. Chesebro, Jr.

Jon Helminiak

Milwaukee, Wisconsin

Copyright © 2025 by Jon Helminiak
All rights reserved.

Photos courtesy of the Robert E. Chesebro, Jr. family.

Published by
HenschelHAUS Publishing, Inc.
Milwaukee, Wisconsin
www.henschelHAUSbooks.com

ISBN: 9798991279192
LCCN: 2025933201

Printed in the United States of America

The Quiet Icon

The Influential Life of Robert E. Chesebro, Jr.

Table of Contents

Foreword i

Preface 1

Introduction 3

Blessed Beginnings 5

The Company 37

Late Bloomers 57

The Next Generation 79

Chief Bob 91

Duty and Obligation 113

Elkhart Lake 129

The Handoff 137

Everywhere and Anywhere 149

Attitude and Inspiration 159

Acknowledgements 163

FOREWORD

This book is about Bob Chesebro, a man who ran a global company, yet made time to be a cause-driven leader in many philanthropic sectors. I have been fortunate in my long career as a YMCA professional to have been mentored by Bob. I am not alone; many other nonprofit executives have been positively impacted by his quiet, yet powerful guidance.

Bob's biography is both needed and important. It's an inspirational story about how one man helped improve the lives of thousands of people in Sheboygan, Wisconsin. It also shows how the family company, Wigwam Mills, remains locally owned and operated—a difficult feat in times of consolidation and buy-outs. Through actions, collaborations, and commitments, Bob Chesebro has positively impacted thousands of "his" employees and many others through his charitable service.

I met Bob in the late 1960s when he served on the Sheboygan YMCA Board of Directors. Like his father and grandfather, he held leadership positions during the Y's major fundraising campaigns. He led by example, and always exceeded his goals.

Sheboygan County has been blessed to have generations of families like the Chesebros who have invested in the community. All of them are accomplished cause-driven leaders who have made an impact by preparing and encouraging people to pursue positive change for all.

I hope Bob's biography will inspire others to do the same.

Donna Wendlandt
Executive Director
Sheboygan, Wisconsin YMCA

PREFACE

Our father has always been fascinated with history. Along with his traditional education at Carleton College, where he majored in history, he has similarly been drawn to literature and film. So it is not surprising that he holds a wealth of historical knowledge related to our family. As is the case with so many families, generations of loved ones pass without leaving much in the way of personal history, told in writing, or even storytelling, which fades over years. We think our father's original intention was to capture and document the full history of Wigwam Mills as he began to embrace his retirement from the business. While the company was his passion, we felt the chronicle of his life was far more worthy, and held things far more interesting.

Throughout the collective journey of writing this book, it seems a Higher Power had something far more meaningful in mind for all of us. The business and our dad are inextricably linked, and Wigwam has been a significant part of his life. Yet when it comes down to it, it is not family business, but the business of family. Robert Chesebro's life is about the strength of family, both the one into which he was born, and the other that he created alongside our mother. Our dad has supported our lineal family as well as a community of family throughout his lifetime, and has done so by embracing his own, unique journey.

The Quiet Icon

Robert Chesebro's path is honorable, humble, and quiet. Yet with significant impact and determination, he made a monumental difference in the lives of others. We hope the reader finds inspiration in these pages, as well as a bit of humor along the way.

Chris Chesebro
Margaret (Chesebro) Newhard

INTRODUCTION

One thing you need to understand about Robert E. Chesebro Jr. is that he is remarkably predictable. All who have known him, and there are hundreds, have seen a man of unusual stability. He's not a person who wandered through life seeking its meaning or contemplating his own purpose. He always knew his destiny, and seldom wavered from that path. Successful people are usually like that. They know themselves well and are immensely comfortable being who they are.

It wasn't always that way. Bob Chesebro was raised in the shadows of a powerful and influential father and uncle. He stuttered, had acne, and was often insecure. Girls and dating terrified him. He admitted, "I was a late bloomer."

There was also the specter of Wigwam Mills, a successful woolen hosiery company founded by his grandfather in 1915. Growing up, Bob's father was the corporate boss, and youthful Bob wondered if he'd eventually take over. The subject was seldom discussed, but from birth, Bob's life and Wigwam Mills were powerfully intertwined. Around town, the Chesebro and Wigwam names were one in the same.

At some point, Bob Chesebro began authoring his Wigwam biographical memoirs. He tapped out a few chapters on a laptop computer and sorted through long-forgotten photos. Writing about oneself can be difficult for someone who is naturally humble. The writing stopped, and Bob contacted me.

We met at his Sheboygan bluff-top home overlooking Lake Michigan. It was fitting that Bob's biography began here, in the house purchased by his parents in 1945 when he was eight years old.

America likes to believe that it produces men and women who embody values of faith, work, charity, and family. The truth is that men like that are rare, not only in America but almost anywhere. They infrequently pass among us. When they do, their story is worth telling. Bob Chesebro is one of those men.

BLESSED BEGINNINGS

One of the stories that Bob Chesebro Jr. likes to tell is about how a local judge once told his father that he'd never amount to anything. Nobody is sure why young Robert Sr. was in a courtroom, but there is no doubt that hearing those words changed him.

Being declared a failure at a young age can impact a boy in two ways. He can believe it will come true, or he can prove it wrong. Robert Sr. chose the latter, and for the rest of his life, the chip on his shoulder influenced almost everything he did.

Like most children, Robert E. Chesebro Jr. was profoundly impacted by his parents. Born on June 15, 1937, in Sheboygan, Wisconsin, Bob was the first child of Helen and Robert Chesebro Sr. A second son, Jim, was born two years later.

The Chesebro residence was a two-story wooden home on 1220 N. 7th Street in Sheboygan. It was a comfortable, middle-class neighborhood with manicured lawns, stately elm trees, and church-going neighbors. American flags hung from poles on front porches. At Christmas time, the Chesebro living room sparkled with a large, lighted tree. Colorful stockings hung above the fireplace. It was a comfortable setting for young Bob and Jim, who were loved and protected by their parents.

The Quiet Icon

Bob's father was a steadfast Congregationalist who knew what he liked and disliked. There were rights and wrongs and not much in between. Gray areas were not part of his thinking. He was born into an upper-class family who owned the Hand Knit Hosiery Company. Founded in 1905, Hand Knit, as it became known, made wool socks, sweaters, and related accessories that kept people warm in the winter. Their Wigwam sock brand became a national bestseller.

Around 1922, Robert Sr. dropped out of New Bedford Textile College in Massachusetts to help his father, Herbert, in the business. He worked his way up in the company, eventually inheriting both the hosiery company and the presidency at a young age. It was a prestigious job, and he drew a comfortable salary.

Bob's father worked relentlessly and had demanding standards. He could be funny and charming one moment and bossy the next. He was well connected, and despite his English heritage, he spoke some German. An ample supply of bourbon and scotch was kept in the basement. He donated to and volunteered for many local causes and was a member of the Masons and the Elks and Rotary clubs.

Robert Sr. was a typical 1930s man. He labored long hours and sometimes ate dinner alone. His relationship with his sons was protective, but distant. There were no heart-to-heart conversations and no hugs. The words "I love you" were absent.

"I never talked to my father about deep things, or why he did this or that," recalled Bob Jr. "He was a good dad and loved me, but not in an obvious way. It was something I just sensed. I really wasn't that close to him. I was much closer to Mom because she was more emotionally available."

In 1889, Henry C. married Augusta Bodenstein, and on July 20, 1902, Bob's mother, Helen, was born. in Sheboygan. Her father, Henry C. Prange, was the son of German farmers who settled in Wisconsin in 1848. Like many immigrants, he spoke mostly German at home and in the neighborhood.

Bob's father, Robert Chesebro Sr.

From a young age, Bob's maternal grandfather was determined to succeed. At age 17, he left the family farm and settled in Sheboygan. He found work at a general store as a clerk, janitor, and delivery boy.

Nine years later, in 1887 at age 26, he founded his own shop and named it H. C. Prange. Henry immediately announced he would provide credit to farmers, something the competition didn't offer. His store became wildly popular, and in 1923, a new facility was built to accommodate the flood of customers. The new building was as large as three football fields, making it the grandest store in Wisconsin outside of Milwaukee. It was a sight to behold, the crown jewel of Sheboygan.

The family lived in a three-story home at 617 Erie Avenue, a relatively affluent neighborhood. Helen attended kindergarten at Sheboygan's Trinity Lutheran Church, where the family worshipped every Sunday. She graduated from Sweetbriar College in Virginia and then travelled with a friend through Europe, a luxury in the day. Sometime after returning home, she met Robert Chesebro Sr., and they married in 1936. They honeymooned in Kentucky and visited the iconic Mammoth Cave.

Born a Prange and marrying a Chesebro, Bob's mother was highly regarded. She graciously accepted her standing, dressed stylishly, behaved impeccably, and spoke reasonably fluent German. She played bridge with Sheboygan's noteworthy, drank scotch and soda, socially smoked, and held her own in any conversation. Bob admitted that "Mom was the leader of our family."

Despite her status, Helen Chesebro never looked down on anybody. It just wasn't in her DNA. The family cleaning lady, Mrs. Roth, was a German immigrant who lived with her husband and disabled son in a modest home on Erie Avenue, about a mile away. On cleaning day, Helen made lunch and ate at the table with Mrs. Roth. Bob explained, "Most people in the 1940s didn't do that. Back then, social mingling between upper and lower classes wasn't proper." But the two ladies sometimes sat for hours, chatting in German and often laughing. That memory guided Bob's treatment of others for his lifetime.

The Chesebros were popular and well liked. Eleanor "Tippy" Jung, a family friend, described them as "fine, upstanding, dignified, and respected." Another friend, Fred Heider, recalled, "Bob's parents were very cultured and well-traveled. They went to Broadway shows in New York City and Chicago. They knew that the world was bigger than Sheboygan, Wisconsin."

At the time, Sheboygan remained a city of immigrants who arrived with trunks of dreams and usually empty pockets. The men found jobs in factories, and the women cleaned houses, child-sat, or worked as cooks. The hours were long and the pay minimal. Families lived in one-room boarding houses until there was enough money to buy a small home. Milkmen made their rounds by horse and carriage, and furnaces burned coal.

The *Sheboygan Press* brought all the daily news, and vendors hawked the latest edition on street corners, inviting the townsfolk to pay a nickel for the latest scoops. Headlines touted the mayhem created by Bonnie and Clyde and John

Robert E. Chesebro Jr. with his parents, Helen and Robert Chesebro Sr. in 1938.

The Quiet Icon

Dillinger. The sports pages had columns about the surging Chicago Cubs or the racehorse phenome, Seabiscuit. Globally, Hitler's army had marched into Austria, and the dictator was eyeing Poland.

At the movie theatres,[1] people lined up to see Clark Gable, Myrna Loy, and Gary Cooper. On the radio, Orson Welles' reading of "The War of the Worlds" caused a temporary national panic.

Such was the world into which Robert E. Chesebro Jr. was born in 1937. The American dream awaited him, as it did for anyone willing to work for it. Through risk and determination, his parents and relatives had achieved those pinnacles of American success.

But Robert Jr. was guaranteed nothing. His proving ground would be long, and at times arduous. Young Bob Chesebro Jr. may have been gifted a noble birthright, but what he did with it would be entirely up to him.

* * *

Although born into a family with gravitas, Robert Chesebro Jr.'s youth was like that of most other Sheboygan boys.

In primary school, he walked or rode his bicycle to nearby Grant School.[2] Around noon, both Bob and father went home for dinner, the largest meal of the day. At recess, sometimes he and his friends Willis Wick, Fred Heider, and

---

[1] There were four movie theatres in Sheboygan: the Majestic, Rex, Strand, and Wisconsin.

[2] The Grant School originated from the First Ward School, which opened in 1892. It was renamed the Ulysses S. Grant Elementary School in 1912. In 1969 the original 1892 structure was demolished to make way for the present school, which retains the same name.

David Witter played marbles or launched their bikes over small jumps to see how high they could fly.

Recess was never long enough, and some classes seemed like an eternity. Bob was the kid in the back of the room who was just a little bit different. His art teacher, Mrs. May Wagner, terrified him. Bob remembered, "I was a late bloomer, and she treated me as such. It was just the way it was." He cowered around his civics teacher who once threw scissors at him.

In Bob's era, school discipline could be traumatic. Students who talked during class could be required to stand in front of the room and write a hundred times on the blackboard "I will not talk in school!" Or the child might be told to stand on one foot and contemplate his or her misdeeds. One boy recalled his teacher picking him up by the ears and parading him around the classroom as an example

Brothers Jim and Bob Chesebro with their dog, Chiri, around 1948.

The Quiet Icon

of a hoodlum. Today, these methods would be considered abusive, but in light of the period, they were mostly effective.

Outside of school, Bob joined the Cub Scouts, attended birthday parties, and went skiing in the winter. On Saturday mornings, he watched a newfangled device called the television. Children across the nation were captivated by shows like "The Adventures of Superman," "Howdy Doody," or the "Cisco Kid." Sometimes Bob and his brother Jim joined their father at the Hand Knit Hosiery plant and played in bins of socks at the warehouse. On Sunday mornings, the family worshipped at both the First United Lutheran or the First Congregational churches.

There were also outings to Prange's Department Store, the most glittering attraction in town. Bob's uncle, Carl Prange was the CEO, and he held as much clout as the mayor, maybe even more. From his top floor office, he managed millions of dollars of inventory and hundreds of employees. There were branch stores in Green Bay and Appleton, but the Sheboygan headquarters was where the retail magic was planned.

One didn't visit Prange's on a whim. Going required planning. The concrete bastion boasted four stories occupying one square block on the corners of 8th Street and Wisconsin Avenue. Advertising promoted 120 categories of items, including a drapery shop, bridal salon, fur salon, appliances, camera shop, and a hat bar. A soda fountain on the mezzanine served food to hungry shoppers seated amidst their bags of purchases. Bob's mother had a weekly appointment at the hair salon.

The H.C. Prange Department Store was grandest store in Wisconsin outside of Milwaukee. It was a sight to behold, the crown jewel of Sheboygan.

Inside, hot water radiators warmed the premises in winter, and mechanical fans cooled them in the summer. The ceiling was lined with exposed pipes, and beams were punctuated by bare fluorescent bulbs. Narrow aisles, resembling foot paths, invited customers to investigate the latest merchandise within easy reach. There was so much inventory that a shopper could hide for days and never be found.

At Christmas, Santa Claus sat on a sparkling throne and listened to children's gift wishes. Through snow-flocked windows, shoppers saw Lionel trains circling presents of toasters, sweaters, and toys. The scent of caramel corn, sweetened in big copper kettles near the doors, wafted around the entrance. There was even a grocery store with most everything needed for the kitchen.

Prange's was the pride of the Sheboygan, a big city department store in small town Wisconsin. Milwaukee had Gimbels and Boston Store, and Chicago boasted Marshall Field's. But Prange's was equally amazing in its own, local way.

It was also part of a family secret. The Chesebro men never bought suits from Prange's. In their opinion, the quality was just not good enough. Bob's father purchased his business attire in Chicago, and young Bob's sport coats and slacks were acquired in Milwaukee. Bob's mother removed the store labels so nobody would know.[3]

Raised in the auras of Wigwam Mills and Prange's, young Bob Chesebro was profoundly impacted by his father and uncle. They were hardworking men who had reached pinnacles of business success. They received awards, were recognized in public, and their names were in the newspapers. This could be intimidating to young Bob, who sometimes wondered if he could ever be as triumphant as they were. And what if he didn't want to be like them? Such were the feelings of a shy and often insecure boy.

---

[3] In 1992, Younkers, Inc., purchased the H. C. Prange Company's 25-unit department store division and the stores were renamed "Younkers." In 2006, Younkers was purchased by Bon Ton Holding, Inc., who operated the stores under their Boston Store banner. In 2015, the flagship original Prange's building on 8th street and Wisconsin in Sheboygan was razed.

Shoppers at Prange's could explore four floors of merchandise. There was also a soda fountain and grocery store.

* * *

From Memorial Day to Labor Day, Wisconsinites live outdoors. Freed from the shackles of icy winters, summer sunshine restores energy and spirit.

Most summers, Bob and his family lived at his mother's family cottage on Elkhart Lake, about a thirty-minute drive from Sheboygan. One could also get there via the "interurban," a trolley that ran between the two towns.

The Prange cottage was among a row of lake homes owned by notable Sheboygan families, most of whom knew each other. For Bob and his brother, Jim, summers at the lake were carefree. Friends visited and spent the night, the days were long and sunny, and the outdoor grill was usually smoking with the aroma of brats and other meats. Bob recalled, "We'd go swimming, paddle boats, sail, and even waterski behind Dad's small outboard boat. When I was a little older, we also drank a lot of beer there."

For all of its magnetism, life at Elkhart Lake could be insular. Most boys didn't have the luxury of a summer lake house, so Bob's mother introduced her sons to different places and people. Bob attended a summer music camp in Denver, and also Camp Manito-wish in far northern Wisconsin. Occasionally, the Chesebros loaded the family sedan and headed to parts unknown. The U.S. interstate system didn't exist, so Bob's father navigated along two-lane highways that were mostly narrow with small shoulders.[4] Destinations included Boston, the Whiteface Mountain in New York, Coney Island, and fishing in Canada.

Dad was the family disciplinarian, but Bob never got into much trouble. He was well behaved in school and at home and avoided conflict. His worst offense, and the only one, happened in grade school when he spit on a man through an open car window. The victim chased Bob through the neighborhood but never caught him. Bob couldn't remember why he spat, and his parents never learned about the incident.

---

[4] Prior to President Eisenhower signing the Federal Highway Act in 1956 (which began the construction of the nation's interstate system), states set their own speed limits. Most drove 50 to 60 mph, which felt safe.

Blessed Beginnings

The 1953 Chesebro Family Christmas card. Pictured are Helen Prange Chesebro, Robert Chesebro Sr., Robert Chesebro Jr., and Jim Chesebro.

Bob attended Sheboygan North High School, one of two secondary schools in town. He was a good student but self-conscious, his natural shyness exacerbated by stuttering and acne. He avoided girls and kept to himself, although he joined the golf team and played clarinet in the band and marching band. Bob recalled, "That was excellent musical training for me. We played excerpts from the *William Tell* and *1812* overtures, and the *Barber of Seville*."

During football season, he sat in the bleachers and rooted for his team, the North Golden Raiders. In the classroom, he excelled in English, German, and history but struggled with math and chemistry. Bob and his mother

The Quiet Icon

liked his history teacher, Miss Bernice Scott. Bob said, "She seemed to understand that I was different, and Mom appreciated her gentle demeanor and how she treated me."

Bob owned a car, and his classmates took notice. Most Sheboygan kids didn't drive their own vehicles, so Bob enjoyed the popularity that came with having his own set of wheels.

The "Blue Beetle" was a 1937 Ford Sedan that originally belonged to his grandmother. It had a stick shift on the floor, four doors, running boards, and a shade in the back window. Its flat-head, eight-cylinder engine provided

Pictured is the Chesebro home on Euclid Avenue in Sheboygan, near Lake Michigan. Bob's parents bought the house in 1950, and Bob's family moved there in 2004.

jackrabbit quickness. His friend Fred Heider said, "We'd cruise around town and go out for hamburgers. When I ran for student council president, we decorated the car with campaign signs and drove around town. Bob and his car were at the core of my campaign, and we won."[5]

Bob drank beer in high school, and even at home when his parents said, "go ahead and have a drink." The legal drinking age was 21, but students knew that if you looked 16, you could get a beer most anywhere. He drank with his pals on weekends and at Elkhart Lake in the summertime. The resort town boasted a robust nightlife, including live music and comedians. Bob was often there, hanging out in the back with his buddies, sipping beer and scanning the crowd for girls and friends.

Around his junior year of high school, Bob contemplated college. His grades were above average, so he had ample choices. Big schools like the University of Wisconsin seemed too large and impersonal. He liked the idea of a small college, and his parents and

Bob graduated from Sheboygan North High School in in 1955.

---

[5] The election team named themselves "The Blue Beatles" and consisted of classmates Fred Heider, Roger Schnell, Willis Wick, David Weider, and Bob.

high school guidance counselors agreed. They settled on Carleton College, a private liberal arts college in Northfield, Minnesota. With an enrollment of about 800 students, it offered a low student-professor ratio, and a close-knit student body, both of which Bob needed to flourish.

Meanwhile, Bob's brother, Jim, was offered a scholarship at the University of Rochester in New York. Most parents would be pleased with financial support, but the elder Chesebro patriarch exclaimed, "Hell, no. Don't rob that scholarship money from somebody who needs it. I can afford to pay for your college."

Jim majored in biology and chemistry, and eventually graduated from medical school at the University of Rochester school of Medicine and Dentistry in 1966. He fulfilled his medical internships and residencies, served as a medic during the Vietnam conflict, and became a successful and respected cardiologist and researcher. Jim and his wife, Christine, raised three sons and a daughter.

Bob explained, "Jim was as devoted to medicine as I eventually was to socks. Although he was a company shareholder, he never showed interest in joining the Wigwam firm. As adults, we'd occasionally see each other, but we were not close."

* * *

On arrival day at Carleton College, the dean of students addressed the freshman class. He told them to look at the person to the left and the right. One of them wouldn't make it to their sophomore year. Carleton was a tough school, and 30 percent would go home after just one semester. Bob vowed that he wouldn't be one of them, knowing that failure would stain the Chesebro Family legacy.

Bob lived in the dormitories with different roommates. One of them dressed only in black and had peculiar mannerisms that kept Bob distant. Then he met John Wilder from Edina, Minnesota. "I liked Bob right away, even though we were different," recalled Wilder. "I was outgoing and talkative. Bob was calm and reserved. But he had a great sense of humor and was fun to be with." The two became immediate friends in an "odd couple" sort of way.

On campus, Bob was liberated from parental oversight and the microscope of Sheboygan life. College presented seductive temptations such as beer drinking, downtown bars, weekend parties, and the lure of the opposite sex. Being at Carleton was a license for good times.

Fred Heider claimed that this boosted Bob's confidence. "He made a lot of lifetime friends at Carleton, and the social life was good for him."

Still, Bob was different from the typical Carleton student. "He had an aluminum box, about the size of a small suitcase," Heider explained. "Every week, he put his dirty clothes into that case and mailed it home. The box was returned to him with clean clothing, all perfectly ironed, starched, and folded. There was even a box of cookies. Nobody else at Carleton did that."

Like many adolescent boys, Bob had acne. For treatments, he took a 56-mile cab ride to the Mayo Clinic in Rochester, Minnesota. Heider found it remarkable that Bob got the best medical care on a regular basis.

On autumn weekends, Bob went pheasant hunting in the nearby fields. He brought his kills to the resident hall chefs, who gladly prepared them. Bob was also a connoisseur of beef tongue, which he prepared himself and served with rye bread. He admitted, "My friends didn't like that too much, but to me, it was a delicacy."

The Carleton experience was formative in Bob's life. At an alumni reunion, Bob gave a speech in which he reminisced about the fun times he had. Fred Heider recalled, "He was really funny, and had his classmates in stiches. He was a stand-up comedian."

* * *

During his junior year of college in 1958, Bob and a couple of pals, Kirk MacKinnon and Norris "Norrie" Jones, decided to visit Europe. MacKinnon was a clean-cut, lanky kid whose mischievous grin made you think he secretly knew that something funny was about to happen. Norrie had crewcut black hair and a dark beard that covered his neck and cheeks. He had no moustache, and wore thick, black-rimmed glasses.

The guys knew it might be their last chance to see Europe before graduation and taking jobs. They scratched out a rough itinerary including the U.K., France, Belgium, Germany, Spain, and Italy. They agreed that the details could be figured out when they arrived.

In June, the trio boarded the Greek liner S.S. *Arkadia* in Montreal, Canada. After navigating a maze of hallways and promenades, the young men found their cabin, a basic accommodation with bunk beds, a tiny bathroom, desk, and chair. A round, brass window could be unlatched to admit the sea breeze. They deposited their bags and went exploring. None of them had experienced a ship of this magnitude, and it seemed huge, even overwhelming. Squeezing between passengers, they discovered fancy restaurants, bars, dance floors, a movie theatre, billiards hall, library, and even a smoking lounge. They also spotted attractive young women who they hoped might be single.

This was almost too good to be true. The S.S. *Arkadia* was an amusement park of adult entertainment, a floating temple of maritime engineering that presented a world of fun. For young men on the cusp of responsible adulthood, temptation was everywhere. With no classes, exams, deadlines, and early alarm bells, there was nothing to restrain them. Six days of hedonism waited.

On deck, Bob and his cohorts watched the burly, tattooed crew cast aside the *Arkadia*'s mooring ropes. Well-wishers on shore waved white handkerchiefs, and the great ship's horn bellowed farewell. When the harbor vanished into the distance, the young adventurers got to work.

The first stop was the bar at the stern of the ship. The drink menu offered fruity options like the "Sea Nymph," the "Shark Tail," or "The All Aboard," which contained no fewer than eight different liquors. They kept it simple and ordered beers, and then more. Kirk wanted to check out the dance hall, which had nightly live music. Bob thought they should first eat dinner, but Kirk disagreed, preferring to arrive at the dance before the best girls were taken.

"Shouldn't we put on a coat and tie?" suggested Bob. After changing clothes and splashing on a bit of cologne, the young men strutted into the dance hall. The band was in full swing, playing a rendition of Elvis Presley's 1956 hit song "Heartbreak Hotel." Beneath the crystal chandeliers, partiers gyrated on the wood dance floor. The young men

The Quiet Icon

joined them and eventually retreated to their bedroom at the glow of sunrise.

They awoke hungover. After stuffing themselves at brunch, they napped, and then repeated the previous night's activities. After six days at sea, the *Arkadia* reached port at Cork, Ireland. The land was green and rolling, just like Bob had seen in the brochures. Tugboats nudged the great ship toward its berth while the passengers gathered on deck, hoping to spot a loved one among the hundreds waiting on shore.

At 5:00 a.m., nobody was waiting for Bob, Kirk, and Norrie when they disembarked. Kirk said, "Bob, you look sick." He was indeed ill, the victim of excessive food, drink, and little sleep. Bob and Kirk boarded a train for Dublin (Norrie decided to hitchhike), where they found the Sligo Hotel, and walked up three flights of stairs to their gloomy room. A communal bathroom and sink was down the hall. Bob collapsed and fell asleep on a straw mattress. It took him a few days to recover.

From Dublin, the group flew to Edinburgh, Scotland, and splurged for a hotel room with its own bathroom and running water. The Scottish weather matched its rainy reputation, so the trio escaped into the pubs and tested the scotch whiskies, drinking them neat with no ice.

They toured the countryside by bus. The guide, dressed in a kilt and white knee socks, stood near the driver, held a microphone, and prattled on about Scottish history, local landmarks, and the fact that some Scottish families had lived in the same town for thousands of years. Outside there were lots of sheep, pastures, and endless stone walls a few feet high. It was foggy and rainy.

Blessed Beginnings

The next day, they left Scotland for London. Bob claimed that his father knew a member of Parliament, a Rotarian, who might be willing to meet them.

The train ride from Edinburgh to London took about five hours. At Waterloo Station, Bob phoned the Parliamentarian, Cyril Osborne, who invited them to lunch the following day. He told Bob to meet him at the Westminster Palace, the home of the two houses of the British Parliament. Sir Osborne, as he was known, would wait for them at the main entrance.

This was unexpected. Bob never thought that Sir Osborne would offer a lunch gathering at the most powerful government house in the United Kingdom.

Ragged and unshaven, the trio found a nice hotel and the next morning, transitioned from vagabond travelers into young professionals wearing sport coats and ties. They boarded a taxi and arrived at Westminster, where tourists were snapping photos of the towers, the stonework, the gardens, the brass gates, and of each other.

Sir Osborne greeted them and escorted them to the opulent dining hall. He asked them about their travels, schooling, and then spoke about current issues. Bob recalled the meeting as "very educational," although much of the impact was simply lunching with a Parliamentarian in the Westminster dining room.[6]

Days later, the group took a ferry across the English Channel to France and boarded a train to Paris, where a

---

[6] Sir Cyril Osborne was Justice of the Peace for Leicestershire, and British Conservative politician, who served as Member of Parliament (MP) for the Louth constituency in Lincolnshire from 1945 to his death in 1969 at age 71.

brand-new Volkswagen microbus awaited them, courtesy of the father of a friend who was supposed to be on the trip but couldn't make it. As the dealer handed over the keys, Bob asked, "Who wants to drive?" Nobody volunteered, so Bob took the wheel. He had no fear of the Paris traffic, reading maps, or deciphering the French language.

The microbus was also a convenient place to sleep and eat. They bought blankets, arranging everything just right so there was enough room for three bodies to lie down. It was tight, but it worked.

Freed from train schedules and taxi cabs, the group mapped out their minibus destinations. Bob said the French Rivera was supposed to be gorgeous. Norrie wanted to run with the bulls in Pamplona, Spain. Kirk badly wanted to eat

Bob Chesebro and Kirk McKennon stand beside the Mediterranean Sea during their overseas trip in summer 1958.

Italian food, his favorite. Everyone agreed that Italy would be worthwhile, so Bob added the Leaning Tower of Pisa, Rome, Florence, and Venice to the list.

It was an ambitious itinerary, but they had a minibus, ample time, and money left over. Bob drove the Volkswagen more than 2,000 miles without an accident or incident. The young men saw everything they wanted to see, with the exception of the World's Fair in Belgium.

The 1958 World's Fair was a global extravaganza. Held in Brussels and named "Expo 58," the theme was the "evaluation of the world for a more humane world." The motto was inspired by faith in technical and scientific progress, as well as post-war debates over the ethical use of atomic power. Forty-two nations erected buildings and installed high-tech exhibits that touted their countries. The grounds were so expansive that a person could spend a week there and not see everything. More than 41 million people attended.

Bob pronounced the show "amazing," but exhausting. After a few days, he flew alone to West Berlin, Germany, wanting to experience a city divided by the Cold War. There, he chatted with people in cafes and entered Communist East Berlin via "Checkpoint Charlie."

After two months abroad, everyone was ready for home.[7] In mid-August 1958, they returned on the same ship,

---

[7] Norrie Jones went on to earn an MS in geology from the University of Minnesota, and a PhD from Virginia Tech. In 1968, he joined the faculty of the University of Wisconsin – Oshkosh and served as Chair of the Department of Geology from 1981-84 and 1996-1999. Kirk MacKinnion graduated from the University of Michigan Law School and died in a freak accident at a young age.

the S.S. *Arkadia*. Onboard, Bob met a pretty American girl who was attending a private university on the East Coast. A romance ensued, and the voyage passed too quickly.

The European adventure bolstered Bob's wanderlust. During spring break, he and some pals drove to Florida in old Mercury with bald tires. They swam, drank beer, and took a boat to the Bahamas. After graduation, he was on a windjammer cruise that began in Puerto Rico and stopped at the islands of Martinique, St. John, and St. Lucia. The cabins were small, stuffy, and hot, so Bob slept outside on the deck. Within the confines of a small boat, he was forced to socialize and mingle with the other travelers. He was getting better at that, but his stuttering, still not fully resolved, made him a reluctant conversationalist.

All of these journeys – Europe, Florida, and the Caribbean – enhanced Bob's confidence. Discovering new places was exhilarating, but the true reward was that he could be himself without judgment. The anonymity that came with strange territory was liberating. The eyes of family, school, or small-town locals were refreshingly absent.

Most of all, he learned that he could survive, and maybe even prosper, on his own. Travel boosted his self-esteem in ways that schools never could.

* * *

In 1959, Bob graduated from Carleton with a degree in history and a minor in economics. Lacking further plans, he went home to Sheboygan. That summer, his mother phoned him and told him that his father had suffered a minor stroke, was temporarily incapacitated, and recovery would take six months. He was just 56 years old.

Bob wondered what to do next. So far, his life had been a progression of expectations, primarily education. With a college diploma, he needed to secure a job.

The world into which Bob graduated had vastly changed since his birth in 1937. In his short lifetime of 21 years, the nation had recovered from an economic depression and endured two wars. Now, in the late 1950s, America was at peace and life was good again. The economy was robust, rock n' roll was a music sensation, most everyone owned a car, and interstate expressways were being built that enabled drivers to get places in record time.

Despite the national calm, the Pentagon generals, all of whom had lived through World War II, were preparing for more storms. They believed the world was governed by an aggressive use of force. Another Hitler could emerge at any time and the United States needed to be ready. The Soviet Union had just crushed a revolution in Hungary and leader Khrushchev was considered a rogue imperialist. Mother Earth was a dangerous place.

Defending freedoms required a robust military, so in the 1950s, men between the age of 18 and 25 were required to register for the draft. If your number was chosen, conscripts began a new life in the armed forces. This was patriotic duty, but also frightening in an era when most everyone had lost a friend or loved one in recent wars.

Alternatively, young men could volunteer for the military reserves. That required six months of active duty and then five years of reserve duty for a couple of weeks

The Quiet Icon

each summer. So in 1959, Bob Chesebro raised his right hand and pledged allegiance to the United States Marine Corps. He recalled, "I enlisted in the reserves because I didn't want to be drafted and go full time into the service. The process was easy, and the Marines were happy to have me."

The timing was right. At age 21, Bob Chesebro Jr. didn't really have anything else to do.

* * *

It's possible that no branch of the military is more respected than the Marine Corps. A marine might be the closest thing to Superman, and even the caped wonder never achieved like a Marine. From the Battle of Belleau Wood to Iwo Jima, the Marines have earned their legendary toughness. When Germany questioned America's will to fight in World War II, President Roosevelt said he would "Send the Marines" to show them otherwise.

In summer 1959, Bob was sent to Parris Island, South Carolina, the first stop for all Marine recruits. Since 1915, the island has been a colander for young men who desired to be the best. At Parris, Marine aspirations are either rewarded or crushed. Even today, the headshots of Parris Island leaders show them with stern, unsmiling expressions. The island is a serious, demanding place.

Upon arrival, they shaved Bob's head and assigned him to a platoon with a surly drill sergeant who called him "Four-eyes" because he wore glasses. Three months of rigorous training then began.

Blessed Beginnings

The platoon awoke at 5:00 a.m. The men shaved, dressed, and made their beds to perfection. Breakfast was served before sunrise. During the day, they marched for hours under the hot South Carolina sun, endured calisthenics, classes, and chores. Drill sergeants yelled just inches from their faces.

One day, Bob awoke sick with a fever. His sergeant told him, "When you die, let me know, and we'll talk about it." Bob struggled through the day but didn't perish. Lights out was at 9:00 p.m., but Bob never had enough sleep. He said, "During the day, I learned to take a quick nap standing up."

After three months at Parris Island, Bob was sent to Jacksonville, North Carolina, the home of Camp Lejeune. Established in 1941, Lejeune trained soldiers in the arts of combat and amphibious assault. "We had a lot of simulated combat exercises in the woods," recalled Bob. "We'd camp out at night, enact strategies to fight enemy platoons, and we were usually cold and wet."

At Lejeune, Bob learned to maintain and shoot a rifle, although he admitted, "I couldn't shoot worth a damn." He flunked marksmanship, probably due to his poor eyesight. Even so, after three months at Camp Lejeune, Bob emerged as a Marine, Private First Class.

The Marines weren't finished. For two weeks each summer, Bob reported to the Marine reserves. At bases in New England, California, Michigan, and Ft. Sill, Oklahoma, he participated in war simulation and endured high-altitude training. There were also monthly weekend meetings in Oshkosh, Wisconsin and simulated "war games" in the

Kettle Moraine State Forest. After five years, his commitment was satisfied.

"The Marines are a serious bunch, and it wasn't always fun," said Bob. "I'm glad I did it and it helped my confidence. I learned how to be a soldier and it toughened me up. I needed that."

* * *

After discharge from the Marines in spring 1960, Bob returned to Sheboygan and moved in with his parents on Euclid Avenue. He offered to pay rent, but his father refused. Although Robert Sr.'s health had improved, Bob assessed the stroke made him "even more hardened, outspoken, and determined." Few believed Robert Sr. could actually get tougher, but he did. Most everyone noticed.

Back home, Bob puttered around town, enjoyed the Elkhart Lake cottage, and contemplated what to do next. His brother, Jim, was committed to becoming a physician, but Bob's career plans remained nebulous. He thought that his father might give him a job at Wigwam Mills, but it was not to be.

Sensing his son was adrift, Robert Sr. phoned a friend who ran a woolen hosiery mill in Laconia, New Hampshire. He asked him if he would help Bob learn how to make hosiery and teach him about knitting machines. The friend agreed, and Bob was encouraged by the arrangement. Maybe, just maybe, his father was grooming him for the family business. Perhaps the stroke heightened his dad's sense of mortality and the need for a family succession plan.

By sending his son cross-county to apprentice, Robert Sr. showed the wisdom of an insightful parent. Were Bob to learn at Wigwam Mills, he would labor under the pressures of being a Chesebro. In New Hampshire, he was just an anonymous young guy there to learn the industry. Without the aura of being the boss's son, it was easier to focus and achieve. It was a winning strategy.

In fall 1960, Bob loaded a suitcase into his brand-new Chevrolet Corvair and headed east to New Hampshire. He moved into a rooming house on Main Street, a few miles from the Belknap-Sulloway Hosiery Mill. There, he was absorbed into the world of knitting machines and yarn manufacturing. The technology fascinated him, and he learned everything he could. He asked questions, learned by observing, and three months later, emerged with an invaluable education.

Armed with this knowledge, Bob drove back to Sheboygan. His father invited him to spend time at the Wigwam Mills plant, where he was mentored by the heads of all the manufacturing departments.

In summer 1961, the elder Chesebro again intervened in his son's life. Bob recalled, "My father got some advice that I should go to graduate school. He thought that it would be good for my career, whatever that might be."

Bob applied to Harvard and the University of Chicago, but eventually chose the University of Michigan Business School. He studied company management, planning, organization, direction, and control. Two year later, he emerged with a master's degree in business administration.

Now 25 years old, Bob needed to settle on a career. Discussions about his joining the business remained infrequent, and it was an awkward subject. The company

The Quiet Icon

had flourished under the elder Chesebro, and he was a proud steward of the legacy gifted to him by his late father, Herbert. The thought of relinquishing leadership, even to his son, was disquieting.

Although Robert Sr. considered his son to be stable, smart, and capable, he remained unconvinced that Bob possessed the "right stuff" to eventually lead the company. The elder Chesebro could be loud, demanding, and impatient. The young Chesebro was more like his mother, gentle and thoughtful. Those were admirable qualities, but the business world could be a battlefield. Effective corporate leaders needed assertive demeanors.

Robert Sr. also feared letting go of everything he had built. His business was like a child; he gave it love, care, commitment, and it often caused sleepless nights of worry. Employees were extended family. Releasing the leadership of Wigwam Mills was frightening. This may explain why Bob's father didn't outwardly encourage him to join the family business. It was a touchy issue.

After graduate school, Bob sometimes joined his father on business trips to New York City. They always stayed in the Pennsylvania Hotel, across from Penn Station. Making sales calls, Bob lugged four suitcases stuffed with samples of Wigwam socks.

One day, at a crowded crosswalk on 7th Avenue, Bob's father said, "So, Robert, what do you want to do in the company? Do you want to sell socks or buy yarn?" At first, Bob wasn't sure how to answer. The subject that had been kept quiet was now fully exposed on the streets of New York.

The question also implied that he would eventually join the family company.

Before the crosswalk light changed, Bob replied, "Dad, I don't want to sell socks or buy yarn. I want to run the company." They walked on in silence, both contemplating the significance of what just happened. The future leadership of Wigwam Mills may just have been resolved on a street more than one thousand miles away from home.

THE COMPANY

In Sheboygan County, the words Chesebro and socks are inseparable. Like Ford and cars, or Kohler and bathrooms, mention one and thoughts of the other appear.

Socks aren't glamourous like cars or a fresh Kohler toilet or bathtub, but they may be more important. Any podiatrist will tell you that healthy feet are the foundation of the entire body. Victims of even minor foot injuries such as blisters or a sprained toe never imagined such misery. Being "grounded" due to a foot malady will wreck the joy in life. Socks are vital to the feet they protect.

The history of Wigwam Mills is a story of risk, reward, achievements, and failures. There are tales of innovation, unique characters, family dynamics, love, and the American dream. Wigwam not only makes socks, but happy people as well. The commonplace slogan "made with love" could apply to every sock that has left the Wigwam Mills factory and its predecessor plants as well.

To current and former employees, Wigwam Mills is family. They use words like "supportive" and "loyal" and speak of their affection for Bob Chesebro. Some, often with tears, tell how they started with the company at age 18 and retired in a leadership position 50 years later. Socks are almost an afterthought.

The Quiet Icon

Everything began in 1891 when the "great-grandfather" company, the Sheboygan Knitting Company, was founded. Its popular "Wigwam" brand sock was a bestseller. This sock was touted as "warmest when coldest, absolutely fast in color and the best hose on the market for the money." Those were powerful selling points for turn-of-the-century families, many of whom endured long winters huddled around coal- or wood-burning stoves. Outdoor workers, particularly the lumberjacks of northern Wisconsin, craved the wool socks and hats that were handmade by the Sheboygan Knitting Company. These men swore that only Wigwam brand socks kept their feet toasty during sub-zero conditions.

In 1904, the Sheboygan Knitting Company factory burned. Months later, former employees created a successor business named the Hand Knit Hosiery Company. One of the founders, 42-year-old Herbert Chesebro, Bob's grandfather, was named president by the board of directors.

Tall, thin, and sporting a neatly trimmed goatee and a bowtie, the dapper Chesebro spoke clearly and directly. He wasn't necessarily charismatic, but people took notice. Chesebro could change the energy of a room just by walking through the door. He had an inner strength that garnered confidence and comfort, as if everything would be all right as long as he was in charge. He was the ideal leader to build a new hosiery company.

Chesebro had a penchant for finance, and he obsessed about keeping the fledgling company profitable. Marketplace savvy, he predicted the demise of the company's largest potential customer, the lumbering industry. Indeed, by 1905,

The Hand Knit Hosiery Company plant in downtown Sheboygan, circa 1920.

the mighty pine forests of northern Wisconsin were mostly leveled and barren landscapes left behind. Soon there would be no more trees to cut, and the Paul Bunyans would no longer need wool socks and hats.

This terrified the board of directors. Some questioned the wisdom of starting a new company when the largest customer was disappearing. Chesebro told them not to worry; the Hand Knit Hosiery Company would remain viable, and even prosper. He planned to diversify the product line and believed the words "Hand Knit" would distinguish them from the competition. He said, "The customer will have visions of our socks and hats being hand-knit by Grandmother, rocking in her chair in front of the fireplace."

This was a marketing mirage but had some merit. In 1909, the Hand Knit Hosiery Company directors cut the ribbon on its three-story brick factory on the corner of Sheboygan's 14th Street and Huron Avenue. Inside, there were no rocking chairs and fireplaces, but many employees were mothers and grandmothers who stitched and sewed socks by hand. Automation was very new and basic, so the words "hand knit" were mostly true.

Chesebro kept his other promise. In a few years, new products like button-up sweaters, athletic socks, and wool bathing suits were introduced. The first sweaters were advertised as "wool coats" and were designed for fashion (the Men's Shaker Knit Polo) and the outdoors (the Men's Hunting Coat). There were even custom-made sweaters for the family pooch.

To embolden the hand-knit imagery, Chesebro insisted that each catalogue highlight this statement:

> *Our products have the 'make good' stuff in there because they're made good all the way through in the same old-fashioned, honest way that Grandmother knits her stockings and mittens.*

The boss's plan was working. Sales boomed, and a new warehouse and office building were built next door to accommodate the growth. The locals discovered that the Hand Knit Hosiery Company offered jobs with fair wages, thanks to this fellow named Chesebro. Devoted customers spread the word about the quality of the company's products.

There was nothing better to keep you comfortably warm and looking stylish to boot.

Chesebro sensed something sensational was happening. Consumers, vendors, suppliers, and employees were becoming like friends and family. Customers wrote him letters, thanking him for making such wonderful mittens, hats, and socks, which they often found beneath the family Christmas tree.

This was entirely different from other companies whose products were less personal. Tables, dishware, sinks, or even the newly invented radio didn't speak to the heart. Warm socks made people feel comfortable and warm. It was something personal. So they wrote letters of praise and asked for more.

A 1921 Christmas card sent to customers from Herbert Chesebro (pictured top row, center) and the Hand Knit Hosiery sales force.

The Quiet Icon

Chesebro recognized the personal connection his company had with its buyers and vendors. It troubled him that he didn't have time to respond to every letter. It was proper etiquette to reply, and not doing so was impolite. If somebody took the time to put pen to paper, it was your obligation to respond.

Knowing his quandary, a staff member suggested that his reply letters could be sent as part of a new marketing plan. Hearing this, Chesebro straightened his bowtie, rose from his wooden swivel chair, and asked for details.

The company needed a catalog with a personal touch. The publication should include a letter from Herbert Chesebro and also simple tips for businesses and households. New and traditional products lines would be featured with a homey flair, commensurate with the hand knit image. When the catalog arrived in mailboxes, customers should feel as if they received a letter from an old friend.

Chesebro loved the concept. The new catalog was named *Ravelings* and mailed monthly. On the cover, *Ravelings* was spelled out with thick, red wool yarn, and below was a drawing of hands knitting a sock.

Inside, customers saw photos of everyday people, young and old, wearing the latest wool styles from the Hand Knit Hosiery Company. Product descriptions were neighborly, with headlines like "For Daddy, Bud, and Sister," suggesting that "it's a common sight these days to see the whole family rigged out in good, comfortable woolen sweaters." *Ravelings*

---

[8] In the 1940s, *Ravelings* changed from a customer catalog into the in-house, monthly employee newsletter.

The Company

In the 1920s, the Hand Knit Hosiery Company wanted customers to have visions of "socks and hats being hand-knit by Grandmother in front of the fireplace." This was a marketing mirage but had some merit. Many employees were mothers and grandmothers who stitched and sewed socks by hand.

reinforced the image of grandmother and her family running the company, probably from a home just around the corner.

Most Hand Knit Hosiery was sold by small, local stores in the Midwest. Customers headed downtown via trolley, horse, and eventually by automobile. Main Street was packed with shops selling almost everything a family needed. Proprietors and customers greeted each other by name, and always with smiles.

Hand Knit Hosiery products also appeared in shopping catalogues sent by huge companies such as J.C. Penny, Sears Roebuck & Company, and Montgomery Ward. Inside the pages, consumers in distant towns could have a big-city shopping experience. No longer did people need to travel to find specialty items. Everything from farm plows to ovens to magic elixirs could be ordered by mail and be delivered to a doorstep. The United States postal service had transformed American consumerism into a convenient, order-by-mail process. For companies like Hand Knit Hosiery, it was a sales revolution.

In 1924, Herbert Chesebro's son, Robert, took a job in the dye house. Coworkers claimed that the thin, feisty 21-year-old mirrored his father's work ethic and determination. Some speculated that someday he might even run the company, but it was too early to tell. Down the road, Robert might want to do something different with his life. Young men don't always want to labor in the shadow of their fathers.

* * *

At breakfast in 1932, Herbert Chesebro felt ill. He collapsed at the table, the victim of a heart attack at age 69. For most, the news of Herbert's passing just couldn't be true. He was a vibrant and popular icon. Men like that just didn't perish.

The death of Herbert propelled the ascension of his son, Robert, to the helm of company in 1936. Only 33 years old, Robert's poise and demeanor were those of an older man. He didn't seem overwhelmed or intimidated by the challenges of running a large company. He had been preparing for this moment, no matter when it happened, since taking a job in the dye house just twelve years earlier. His time arrived sooner than he wanted or anticipated, but that didn't matter now. The moment was here, and he pledged to seize it.

Robert moved into his father's office with the intention of making his own legacy. He wasn't like his dad and would run things his way. Workers admired his intentions, but they waited to see if his words became actions, and hoped for decisions that would advance Hand Knit's fortunes while maintaining the credibility of the Chesebro lineage. It would be a difficult balancing act.

Young Robert began by eliminating peripheral products that were not profitable, such as wool bathing suits. He wanted to focus solely on Hand Knit's sock and glove line, including hunter's mittens and gloves, skating socks, ski socks, scarves, and baseball and football hose. These items were the best in the business, but there was also competition, so Robert insisted that new, innovative items be created and introduced. Department heads gathered and studied the marketplace and consumer trends. There had to be something that the public needed but wasn't yet being produced.

These deliberations reinforced that most of Hand Knit's products met the needs of winter sports enthusiasts, and little was made for summertime activities. Somebody suggested making wool golf-head covers. Soon, colorful sock-like covers adorned the ends of drivers on golf courses nationwide. Buyers could customize them with "knit-in" numbers for easy club identification. Golf-club covers propelled Wigwam into the summer sports marketplace.

Around the same time in the 1940s, Hand Knit introduced Tepee socks. These modified socks had leather soles and heels. They were essentially an indoor slipper-sock, and nobody else made them.

The Quiet Icon

Robert Sr. loved innovative products because they got people talking about his company. He often imagined himself inside the home of a typical American family and asked himself questions. What did they need that wasn't yet made? What could we do to make their lives easier?

The answers didn't always require a new product. Sometimes existing merchandise just needed to be modified. One of those adaptations came after Robert Sr. observed a problem in his own home. On laundry day, it was difficult to distinguish which pair of socks belonged to his sons, Bob and Jim. Even though they were different sizes, the socks all looked alike. Correctly pairing them could be frustrating.

To help, Robert Sr. decided to differentiate sizes by making colored toe seams. Black threads were size 9, green were size 10, red for 11, blue for 12, and orange for 13. Mothers now had a solution to their sock-sorting challenges.

With both fresh and traditional products, Robert Sr. embarked on a nationwide advertising campaign. The company was headquartered in a small town, but by God, their products deserved national attention. Everyone, from Boston to Los Angeles, should know about the merits of Hand Knit hosiery.

Amidst these innovations, the United States entered World War II after the Japanese bombed Pearl Harbor on December 7, 1941. The nation's focus shifted to defeating Germany and Japan and every citizen helped. Sons and brothers went off to war, families grew "victory gardens," and rationing was common. The War Productions Board, established by President Franklin Roosevelt in 1942, directed the conversation of companies from peacetime work

Vogue Magazine featured Wigwam caffettes and anklets on the cover of their August, 1940 issue.

to war needs. Hand Knit Hosiery was pressed into service, and for a time, only produced socks for the Army and the Navy. The noncombat market would have to wait.

Both servicemen and civilians commonly referred to Hand Knit Hosiery products as "Wigwam," the brand name of their popular socks. This made sense; "Wigwam" was

The Quiet Icon

easier to say than "Hand Knit Hosiery," and the image of the Wigwam logo, a teepee, was unique and memorable.

The company stockholders agreed that Wigwam was an enormously popular name. Conversely, the name Hand Knit Hosiery Company seemed cumbersome.

In 1956, the corporate name was officially changed to Wigwam Mills Inc. Robert Sr. announced the transition in the 1957 catalogue by writing, "But only our name changes. Our people, our quality, our sales policies, and above all, our desire to work with you remain the same."

The name Wigwam was now more than just socks. It was the company identity, brand, and logo for everything they made.

* * *

After their exchange in New York City, when Bob told his father that he wanted to run the company, it seemed only a matter of time until he officially joined the Wigwam Mills operation.

In fall 1962, his father gave him a job and named him a vice-president. The label sounded lofty, but Bob defined the job as "VP of Nothing." There was no job description, nobody to supervise, and nothing to manage. His father told him, "Your job is simple. You're going to educate yourself about this business." That meant Bob would be an understudy in every Wigwam department, from buying yarn to manufacturing to packaging and sales. His mentors would be people who were the best in the knitting industry. They were sticklers for perfection, just the way Wigwam wanted.

At some point, Bob was deemed prepared to sell products. He was assigned to Kentucky and Michigan's

Upper Peninsula, retail territories that few wanted. He loaded his car with suitcases of samples and set off. His sales calls were mostly successful. Being a Chesebro helped, but his humility and Midwestern "aw-shucks" personality were naturally persuasive. He came across as the nicest and most trustworthy person around. Bob also knew his product, down to the last strand of yarn. At the end of a sales call, the customer was convinced he was buying the best socks ever made.

Back at the plant, most everyone, except Bob's father, congratulated him for his success. To Robert Sr., his son was merely doing his job. Bob's reward was a paycheck, and perhaps later, some executive duties.

Robert Sr. was neither Bob's cheerleader nor an encouraging mentor. The reason may have been twofold. Either Bob's father was too busy running the company, or he didn't want to show favoritism toward his son. Bob was an employee like everyone else and would be treated as such.

Bob's longtime friend, Fred Heider, explained, "Robert Sr. was a very strict and difficult man to work with. In the beginning, he gave Bob a lot of grief, and had concerns about him. He was reluctant to hand him the company reins."

For all of his business acumen, Robert Sr. was indeed a tough boss. He was short tempered, outspoken, and impatient. If he didn't like something, he'd shout, "Dammit to hell, do it another way!" Gentleness was not part of his makeup. He wore shoes with hard leather soles so people could hear him coming. The soles made a sharp "click-click" on the hard plant floors, and he walked at fast pace. "People would hear his heels and stiffen up," Bob said. "Some loved him, and others were awed and intimidated by him." Cristal Hodges, a former company secretary, said Robert Sr. "was crabby. He'd come storming out of his office and I was afraid of him."

Salesman Don Meszaros said, "Robert Sr. was an old-school type of leader. He would call us on Saturday mornings and ask us where we were. He'd even call us when we were on vacation." Robert Sr. believed that salesmen needed to be obsessed with their jobs, just like he was. Little else mattered, except maybe your family.

Since Bob's working relationship with his father was awkward, so he sought guidance from others. One was Hugh Dales, company secretary/treasurer. Dales was Robert Sr.'s "right-hand man," and was well aware of the boss's quirks and reputation. He told Bob, "You have the patience of a Sphinx with your father." Dales himself was the opposite of his boss, exhibiting a warm and understanding aura that resonated with Bob. Dales became a supportive mentor, and Bob took his questions to him, and left his father alone.

Another mentor was sales manager Carl Zehms, who said, "Bob, you need to be yourself. You can't be like your dad. You're a much different person. Accept who you are and be proud of it. Others need to know you have confidence in yourself."

Zehms' advice subtly reinforced the rumors that Bob would eventually run the company. Most company executives saw promise in young Bob, even if his father seemed indifferent.

***

In 1968, Helen Chesebro emphatically told her husband that it was time for their son to lead Wigwam Mills. She told him, "He is ready," and that the inevitable transition should happen now. Postponing it would add even more stress to everyone, including her. Helen was the family therapist, reassuring Bob that he would eventually take over, and telling Robert Sr. that it was all right to let go.

Bob recalled, "Dad had seen that I knew how to make a quality sock and could also sell them. That, and Mom's insistence, was enough for him." Robert Sr. asked the board of directors to appoint his son as company president. Robert Sr. would retire and become chairman of the board. Bob was 30 years old, his father 65.

Stepping aside, Robert Sr. received due accolades. Everyone agreed that his 36 years of leadership achieved extraordinary results. The company was making more products and employing more people than ever. The name Wigwam had even joined the American lexicon, in the same vein as Crest, RCA, or Corn Flakes. Many kids of the 1960s remember their mothers asking, "Are you wearing your Wigwams?"

The leadership transition was broadly announced. Few were surprised. Most expected this moment but were unsure of the timing. Robert Sr. gave assurances that he would remain involved, but at a distance.

Letters of congratulations piled up on Bob's desk. Well-wishers phoned him at the office and at home. Bouquets of flowers were delivered. He graciously accepted everything, but his stomach was in turmoil. Bob's dream of

The Quiet Icon

Tennis star Pancho Gonzales and professional golfer Billy Casper endorsed Wigwam products.

running the company now appeared to be an overwhelming responsibility.

That anxiety was rooted in Bob's past. Subconsciously he was still the shy, stuttering boy, sometimes uncomfortable around others. Although he was intellectually ready for the big stage, these insecurities still haunted him. As a company employee, few noticed. Under the spotlight of the presidency, his every move would be evaluated.

That scrutiny began on his first official day during his opening address. In front of him were employees and executives, waiting for his opening remarks. He scanned the faces and saw people twice his age. His father was there, and people with decades of experience were watching. Bob looked at his notes and imagined an empty room. He began, "My name is Bob. I'm your new company president." He paused and moved his eyes back to his people. They were smiling.

Bob's remarks were true to his style: simple and straightforward. He was grateful for the opportunity. He acknowledged his father's decades of company devotion. He invoked the company founder and his grandfather, Herbert. He promised to do his best and expressed his gratitude for the opportunity.

Ten minutes later, there was applause. Looking back, Bob recalled, "I wasn't comfortable during that speech. I was nervous. That uneasiness also ignited my stuttering."[9]

Speaking may have been outside of Bob's comfort zone, but learning how to manage a multi-million-dollar business wasn't. Board member Richard Pauls noted that, "Bob had to learn a lot on the job, and he was fortunate that he inherited a period of profitability and growth. The wind was at his back."

Bob bristled when people claimed that Wigwam was flourishing because he was riding business momentum. That may have been partially true, but in Bob's short tenure, the company was growing. He had no interest in maintaining the status quo. In almost every realm, Bob wanted to make things better. His first action was to lengthen Wigwam's sock style 650, a sized cotton sock, by making it one inch

---

[9] Through sheer determination, Bob eventually overcame his stuttering and became an eloquent and humorous public speaker.

The Quiet Icon

In 1970, construction began on the new Wigwam plant, which was the size of 3.5 football fields. A dedication open house was attended by nearly 4,000 people.

longer in the leg. Salesmen were clamoring for the change, and with that minor adjustment, sales increased. He also fired the advertising company and bolstered Wigwam's in-house marketing team.

Through these changes, Bob remained humble and self-aware. When he needed help, he turned to Ralph E. Ross, a consultant with Kurt Salmon and Associates, a management strategy firm with big-name clients in the textile and apparel industry. Ross was an elder statesman, experienced, patient, and wise. They met every few months in Sheboygan or New York. In between, Bob consulted Ross by telephone.

The Company

No subject was too naïve or major, and the relationship evolved into an almost father and son friendship. Together they developed ambitious business plans, marketplace strategies, and created job descriptions for management.

"We became very close," recalled Bob. "The day Ralph died, he called me from his hospital bed."

Ross impacted knowledge and confidence that few others could. His wisdom stayed with Bob for his lifetime, and he often found himself asking, "What would Ralph do?"

By 1970, after only two years as president, sales and staffing increased. Inventory was mounting. The original plant at 14th and Huron, with its brick façade, small offices, and street parking, was obsolete. Wigwam Mills needed more than a building facelift. It needed an entirely new environment.

An ideal new location was found at the Sheboygan Industrial Park. The board of directors approved the purchase of 16 acres, and the architects were told to design a facility with an attached warehouse and dying facility, more offices, fewer walls, ample parking, and meeting rooms. In short, the plant needed to be fully integrated, and the "feel" needed to be clean, modern, and spacious. Finally, it needed to be emblematic of a first-class producer of quality retail products.

In late 1970, construction began, financed by the first $2.5 million industrial revenue bond in Sheboygan. Three years later, the 200,000 square feet plant, the size of 3.5 football fields, was finished. An open house attracted nearly 4,000 people, including the mayor, leading business executives, and the press.

The Quiet Icon

Bob said, "The new building helped our image in terms of being a viable entity. We finally had everything under one roof. It was air-conditioned, and the manufacturing floors were customized to meet department needs. All of that helped attract new people."

Unsaid was that the gleaming new plant represented an era of new leadership. Without the ghosts of the historic plant, Bob could further impact the company culture with his own style and ideas. It was a therapeutic moment, and a fresh beginning, not only for Bob, but for the 400 Wigwam employees.

LATE BLOOMERS

Around town it was well known that Bob Chesebro was a confirmed bachelor. Fred Heider, Bob's classmate from grade school through Carleton College, professed that "the old gang was convinced that Bob would never marry."

There was ample evidence. In his mid-30s, Bob was living alone in a cabin near the Black River, just outside of town. His friend Richard Pauls described him as "a single guy living in the woods, who was known as a bit of a character. Russ Pilling, a Carlton College classmate, labeled Bob as "shy and quiet, not a party boy and a real 'straight arrow.'" Bob himself admitted that "I didn't really mature and get out that much until well beyond college."

There was also that pesky stuttering. It intensified when Bob was in a new and unfamiliar situation, which usually defines a first date. A combination of the stuttering, a reserved personality, and contentment being alone was a perfect storm for permanent Robert Chesebro bachelorhood.

Sometimes that storm abated, and Bob went on a date. Donning crisply pressed shirts and slacks, shiny shoes, and sometimes a necktie, he'd arrive at the girl's home in his Pontiac GTO with a stick shift. If the first meeting was successful, Bob would phone his new affection and invite her out for something adventurous. Dinner and movie was way too boring; it had to be an outdoor activity that required some skill such as biking, skiing, or swimming.

Later in life, Bob told stories of these rendezvous, as if they were the highlights of his single years. These tales could surface in unusual settings. At meetings of the Wigwam Mills sales staff, daughter Margaret remembered her father "always had a story about a girlfriend. Dad would get into long speeches and sidebars about a former girlfriend, telling us about the times he went horseback riding or skiing with 'so and so.' There was little connection to the topic of discussion."

Bob also gave his daughter dating advice. "Dating today is so different from when I was young. Back then you just went out with people and didn't have to be in a strict regime of being with one person. For example, you go on a vacation, and you meet people." Margaret said her father valued those dating years. "He always had a glow and a smile when speaking about them."

Few dates held Bob's interest. His true love was Wigwam Mills, where he often spent weekends and evenings working alone in his office. Women required time and attention, both of which detracted from running a business. He appreciated the personal freedoms of bachelorhood that some of his married friends seemed to envy.

* * *

In the annals of relationships, playing the matchmaker is risky business. Hearing the words "may I set you up on a date" can terrify single men and women. Stories abound about matchmaking calamities, leaving the victims wondering how well their friends really knew them.

Late Bloomers

In 1974, Bob's friend Tom Roenitz began chatting about his sister, Katie. He said, "Bob, my sister Katie is single, and you're single." This got Bob's attention. He knew the Roenitz family well, except Katie. She was six years younger than Bob, so their youthful worlds seldom overlapped. But Tom's words reinforced Bob's desire to know the pretty young Roenitz girl a whole lot better.

About the same time, Tom asked his sister, "If Bob Chesebro asked you to out with him, would you accept?" Katie said she wasn't sure. "He'd have to ask me out first, and then we'll see."

* * *

In the Great Lakes region, where snow and cold are a way of life, the cupid's arrow often strikes during the sultry days of summer. One hot afternoon at Elkhart Lake, Bob Chesebro was hit. It happened after a noon dinner of lamb chops, a Chesebro Sunday tradition.

With a full belly, Bob changed into his swimming suit, walked to the lake, and plunged in. Stroking freestyle, he headed toward the pier of the Roenitz family, just a few houses away. Katie Roenitz was sunning herself on the dock and Bob asked if he could join her. The two chatted for hours, and the scene repeated itself several consecutive Sundays.

Katie asked her sister JoEllen why Bob was swimming to their cottage. She explained that it was probably because Bob liked her, and maybe wanted to date. She didn't tell her that both families, especially the mothers, were hopeful that the two might become romantic. Bob recalled, "Mother was always trying to set me up on dates and be a matchmaker."

Bob wanted to see a lot more of Katie. He admitted that "The more I saw her, the more I liked her. She was a tomboy, and had a vibrant spirit that was different from most others."

When the leaves turned color, seeing Katie wouldn't be as easy as swimming down the Elkhart Lake shoreline. She lived in a secluded environment in Indiana. Her situation would discourage even the most love-struck men, but Bob Chesebro would not be deterred.

* * *

Most everyone in Sheboygan knew of the Roenitz Family because of the family drug stores owned by Katie's father, James.

The business was started in 1892 by Katie's grandfather, Herman Roenitz. It was one of the few pharmacies in Sheboygan. On the gravel road near the storefront, patrons arrived on foot, by horseback, or in carriages. After school and on weekends, James was often in the store, helping out and observing. He noticed that pharmacy work was more than knowing about elixirs and medications. His father spent a lot of time talking to people. Most everyone in the store had a medical issue, and wanted to know what product might cure them.

Pharmacy work during the Great Depression of the early 1930s was financially challenging, and at one time, the family lost their home. Nevertheless, Herman's son, James, decided to become a pharmacist. He attended a pharmacy school in Philadelphia, went home, and learned that his father wouldn't hire him. The business was fully staffed, and

Herman had promised nobody would lose their jobs when his son returned. With his father's support, James began his own pharmacy.

Business was slow until word spread that young James was every bit as competent as his father. Soon he had enough customers, hired staff, and expanded his store offerings. His work ethic was inexorable, and he sometimes spent the evenings in his office.

In 1937, James married Josephine Reiss Knauf. The vivacious Josephine was a physician's daughter, a college graduate, and a schoolteacher. They eventually had seven children, and Katie was the fourth.

Nicknamed "Dodo," Katie's mother was a wise and compassionate person who made everyone feel good. She was smart, a voracious reader, a devout Catholic, and had a zest for travel. "She was a saint," Bob remembered. James and Dodo were well matched. They had equal intellect, similar interests, and Dodo understood life in a medical-related field.

Even with seven living children, (one was lost during childbirth), James Roenitz lived to work. He left home at 7:30 a.m. and promised to be back for dinner. He was usually late. After eating, he did bookwork. When he turned 65, he had no intentions of retiring, but did acquiesce to Sundays off. When he turned 70, he took an entire weekend away. On Monday morning, he was up early and back at the pharmacy.

Bob Roenitz, Katie's youngest brother, said, "Dad loved people, and taking care of them. He was kind, compassionate, and would do things behind the scenes to help many. He

The Quiet Icon

The Robert Roenitz Family is pictured 1954. Top row: Tom (Gus), Jim, JoEllen, Katie. Bottom Row: Josephine, Bob (on lap), Ruth, Chris and Robert.

wanted the best for his employees and customers." He was proud of his business and kept a putty knife above the door to scrape chewing gum off the sidewalk near the entrance.

Katie's sister Chris rembered her father as having a dry sense of humor. She said, "Dad also mixed well with anybody, no matter their life circumstances. He loved knowing and meeting people, and if somebody needed a project done, he'd quietly do it for them."

Like his own father, James had a way with people. Even angry clients were disarmed by the soothing energy of the pharmacy owner. When an irritated customer accused James of overbilling, he sat them down at the soda fountain counter and poured them a cup of coffee. He left and returned with an armful of financial books, opened them, and explained every billing detail. According to Chris Roenitz, "The guy walked out as if he had just seen the Pope."

At its peak, James managed six Roenitz Drug stores.[10] Three of them had soda fountains and lunch counters, and the others were clinic-pharmacies. There were candy counters, shelves of basic medical items, and prescription windows. James visited each store daily, even in the bitter cold of winter. He wanted to be visible and believed the morale of his staff depended upon it. His work ethic enabled him to send all of his seven children to private colleges. His youngest daughter, Ruth, attended St. Colletta, a school for the handicapped.

Chris Roenitz remembered that her parents "were in love their entire lives, and equal partners in everything. They told us that everybody has to take risks in life, so just go do it."[11]

* * *

Catholicism permeated the Roenitz household. Sunday was the most important day of the week. Prayers were said aloud before each meal. Katie recalled, "A statue of Mary sat at the top of the staircase in our house and my siblings and I would pray the rosary in front of it. All seven of us were in various positions on the steps."

Although God was infused throughout the Roenitz home, Katie said, "Mom wouldn't talk about God. Instead, she lived as God would want, and set an example. She

---

[10] The Roenitz Pharmacies were eventually sold to Aurora Health Care.

[11] James passed away in 1988 at age 78. Josephine died in 2004, age 90.

helped the less fortunate and was always there for anybody who needed help." Her sister Chris added, "We went to church no matter where we were, and our brothers were always the altar boys. Mother attended daily mass."

In grade school, Katie attended St. Clement Church School and then graduated from Sheboygan South High School in 1961. She went to college at St. Mary-of-the-Woods, a private, women-only Catholic liberal arts college near Terre Haute, Indiana. The campus fit seamlessly with Katie's Catholic roots, with college literature stating that "the institution pledges its faithfulness to Jesus Christ, Catholic values, and traditions."

Like many small college towns, the St. Mary-of-the-Woods campus was an oasis of majestic trees, manicured lawn, gardens, and even a few ponds. Some of the enormous buildings could intimidate freshmen students, but Katie felt at ease. Her mother and sister JoEllen were alums of the college, and if they could handle it, so could she.

Life on an all-female campus could be stifling, especially for some young women who had dreams of a husband and family. A private men's college was nearby, and dances were occasionally held. Katie attended but preferred to slip into one of the nearby bars for relaxation with her friends.

Except in the summer, she seldom travelled home. She exchanged letters with friends and family. Long-distance phone calls were expensive, and there were no computers or cell phones.

Katie majored in elementary education, and student taught at St. Benedict's Catholic School in Terre Haute. She pronounced the experience "boring and too routine." After class, she'd sit in the neighborhood tavern, order a beer, and prepare the next day's lesson plan.

Katie graduated from St. Mary-of-the-Woods in 1965 with a degree in elementary education. Then she went home to figure out the next years of her life.

* * *

Decisions define a person's life. Choosing a career, spouse, hobbies, children, and lifestyle can create or destroy destinies.

Katie Roenitz in 1965.

At age 24, Katie Roenitz chose an exceptional path. She decided to join a Catholic convent and began her journey toward sisterhood.

Katie remembered, "I told my parents that I wanted to become a Sister of Providence, and Mom didn't like my decision one bit. She wanted me to get married and start a family." But with no marital prospect, Katie confessed that her choice was born of having "nothing else that I really wanted to do." She explained that a nun was sponsoring her and she had already been admitted. That in itself was an accomplishment because convents accept very few candidates. To Katie, it all seemed ordained, and perhaps God's will.

Her mother wasn't so sure. Convents are mysterious places. Nobody is really sure what happens inside of them.

The Quiet Icon

There are no public tours, and the sisters who live there can be reclusive. Entering the sisterhood requires monumental personal sacrifices. Days are devoted to prayer, solitude, quiet, and God. Vows of poverty, chastity, and obedience are required. There are few weekend trips, outdoor activities, or visits with friends and family. Life in the convent, and life in the outside world, are dichotomous.

Yet in 1965, Katherine Mary Roenitz walked through the large wooden doors of the New Sisters of Providence, a Roman Catholic congregation of women near Terre Haute, Indiana. The convent was named after Saint Mother Theodore Guerin, a French sister whose life story rightfully permeates the congregation's legacy and deserves recognition.

In 1840, at age 42, Saint Mother Theodore and five sisters left France for Indiana. Their mission was to attend to the influx of female Catholic immigrants, and Saint Mother Theodore was considered the only woman who could lead and survive the rigors of this challenging journey. The women crossed the Atlantic on a small ship and seasickness prevailed. Sleep was difficult, and the vomiting sisters prayed for survival.

After docking in the New World, Mother Theodore and the sisters took steam trains and horse-drawn wagons to Indiana. Upon arrival, she saw only wilderness and a farmhouse. The homeowners, Sarah and Joseph Thralls, said the area was called Saint Mary-of-the-Woods. They reassured her that many young women lived in the region, although hours away.

Everyone lived together in the small farmhouse. The bathroom was outside. In winter, they used indoor chamber pots. Water came from a pump, and heat from a wood-burning stove. Even so, one sister chronicled that "everything is frozen, even the bread."

Despite the obstacles, Saint Mother Theodore and the sisters built an academy for girls. It was dedicated on July 4, 1841, just eight months after their arrival. It was a monumental achievement built upon prayer, relentless work, and donated funds. Today, the academy continues as Saint Mary-of-the-Woods College, just adjacent to the convent that bears Saint Mother Theodore Guerin's name.

More than a century after its founding, Katie transitioned into the Saint Mother's spiritual world with 50 other women and God. In her tiny room were a window, a bed, and a dresser. She had no roommate, and a communal bathroom was down the hall. Her first impression was that everything was old—old buildings, old nuns, and old furniture.

Life in the convent was structured and restrictive. Katie recalled, "We awakened at 5:00 a.m., dressed, and went downstairs for prayer in the chapel. After breakfast, we did chores, usually cleaning and scrubbing floors. Speaking was forbidden unless necessary, even during meals. Friendships were discouraged since our only devotion was to God." Bedtime was 8:00 p.m.

As a postulant candidate for sisterhood, Katie wore a simple black jumper and veil, and attended classes to help her grow in wholeness and holiness. In her second year, as a novice, she was given a habit and white veil. Prayer intensi-

The Quiet Icon

Pictured is Katie Chesebro dressed in her habit. This photo was taken around 1978, years after she had left the convent.

fied, and Katie was assigned work duties in the office, print shop, woodworking shop, and the infirmary, caring for elderly nuns. "And we were always doing dishes," she remembered.

Katie was also charged with convent maintenance because "they didn't know what to do with me." Since she held a college degree, the nuns thought she could figure things out when something needed repair. Most sisters only held high school degrees.

At the convent, Katie began graduate studies at Indiana State University, working toward a master's degree in sociology and criminology. Her thesis required visits to the Indiana State Women's Prison, a maximum-security facility near Indianapolis. It was one of the most unsavory prisons in the state.

Katie recalled, "My thesis subject was about whether or not prison life helped inmates. I interviewed many prisoners, one-on-one. It was a rough bunch, and they said things to me that were not very nice." The inmates, mostly between 30 and 40 years old, had committed heinous crimes, usually murder. One inmate killed a priest, another murdered her child.

"One night as I was leaving, all the lights went out," said Katie. "I thought to myself 'this is not' good.' It was a scary place to be during the daytime, even more so in the dark. These were very naughty women."

In the end, her thesis determined that prison life didn't help inmates reform. Katie accepted her master's degree from Indiana State University in 1967.

Studies and convent life restrained Katie's naturally rebellious persona, but it didn't end it. She admitted, "I was always known as somebody on the edge of trouble." Her sister Chris said, "Katie always wanted to push the envelope. She marched to a different drummer."

Once time, Katie returned to the convent at 3:00 a.m., tipsy and past her curfew. She staggered to the chapel and bowed her head, which smacked on the floor. Disoriented, she went to the bathroom, then her room. She collapsed on the bed as a friend entered and exclaimed, "Katie, what have you been doing? Your clothes are all over the hallway."

Katie liked the challenge of outsmarting the nuns and getting around the house rules. It was her way of exerting control in a place where most of her life was planned. When Katie broke a rule and didn't get caught, it reinforced her belief that she was just a little bit wiser and street-smart than everyone else in the building.

Some nuns benefitted from Katie's craftiness. She snuck in cigarettes and beer and sold them. "I'd give the handyman money, ask him to buy beer, bag it, and then told him to hide it in the convent junk pile." She retrieved the beer and stored it in the priest's refrigerator, which he never used. The cigarettes came from her father's drugstores, stuffed inside her suitcase after a visit home.

"I made a nice profit selling the stuff."

She also sold fake ID cards. "My younger brothers taught me how to make them, and I was pretty good at it," she recalled. "One day, a college girl came to the convent, saying that she wanted to see me. She seemed nice and sincere, so the elder nuns allowed us to meet."

The girl whispered that she needed a fake ID. Katie told her, "This is a little out-of-line, but I'll tell you what I'll do for you. Come back in a week or so with your photo and name and say that you need to talk to me one more time." The girl returned and Katie slipped her a perfect ID card. "I told her, 'don't ever tell anyone where you got this.'"

Katie may have been the only nun to ever operate a convent beer dispensary and a fake ID print shop. It may not have been the holy thing to do, but in a way, she was simply using the special gifts God gave her.

* * *

Single men don't usually fancy women living in convents. The nuns take vows of poverty, chastity, and obedience, the three evangelical counsels of Christian perfection. This is not the stuff that excites bachelors. Yet Bob Chesebro was not deterred.

Terre Haute, Indiana, is about a 3.5 hour drive from Sheboygan. Bob often had business in Chicago, or according to Katie, "monkey business." They would meet at the Drake Hotel, go out for dinner, and sometimes ride bikes along the lakeshore. Bob admitted, "We had a lot of good times in Chicago."

Between visits, Bob called Katie at the convent. A single phone was shared by everyone, and when a sister answered, Bob identified himself as "Father Bob" and asked to speak with Sister Katie. Katie spoke softly on the telephone, hoping nobody would discover that the call was from a male suitor, and not a holy father.

With each phone call, Katie became more uncomfortable. She finally told Bob not to phone her anymore. It just wasn't right, especially after he had been drinking. Then she told him, "Bob, I'm not going to leave the convent for you. If I decide to leave, it's because I don't want to do this anymore."

Bob stopped calling, but he didn't end his pursuit. He and Katie went skiing near Montreal, Wisconsin, and stayed with her brother. During another date at the Milwaukee Zoo, somewhere near the elephants, Katie grabbed Bob's arm and said, "Bob, I don't want to see you anymore until I make a decision to leave the convent." Bob said he understood and would wait for her decision.

In 1976, Katie had completed eight years of convent life. She had performed well, despite her free-spirited penchant for trouble. Her superiors believed she would make a fine nun and encouraged her to take her final vows. The finish line was near, but Katie hesitated. Final vows are solemn, perpetual, and serious, including a pledge to relinquish all worldly possessions including property, estates, endowments, and inheritances.

Word spread that Sister Katie Roenitz was reconsidering her life path. Most thought it a rumor; it seemed implausible that Katie would discard years of training for a different future. To find out, Mother Superior met with Katie in her dark office adorned with crucifixes and paintings of Jesus. She said, "Katie, you'd be a good nun and an asset to the community, and we hope you'll fulfill your vows and live here with us."

Katie respectfully told her that she had decided to leave. Mother Superior held Katie's hand and told her she was disappointed. She had hoped that Katie would become a nun. A personal plea from Mother Superior was not to be taken lightly, but Katie was firm. Her future would be elsewhere.

That decision was likely made months ago and was not impulsive. Looking back, Katie said, "I decided I didn't want to spend my days with a bunch of old ladies." It was that simple. She claimed that Bob had nothing to do with it.

Bob said, "During the two years we dated, Katie couldn't decide if she wanted to stay in the convent, or not. She really didn't know what to do with her life. I convinced her that life would be better on the outside."

Katie didn't leave the convent for Bob, but his advice likely reinforced her conclusion. Katie packed her belongings and left through the same wooden door that she'd entered nearly a decade earlier. During that time, she had only seen her family occasionally. The outside world seemed fresher, brighter. With the veils of restrictive convent life lifted, Katie could be herself again.

Inside the convent, Katie learned more about God, life, and perseverance. These lessons would remain with her, and years later, they would help save her life.

* * *

During a summer sunset at Elkhart Lake, sitting close to each other on the cottage porch, Bob asked Katie to marry him. She didn't answer. Instead, she pointed at Bob's shirt pocket and asked him about a folded sheet of paper. "Do you have questions you want to ask me first?"

Bob nodded and unfolded the paper. He read a list of his personal "wife criteria," such as being fun, smart, and having common sense. Katie listened and finally said, "I think it's a good idea to get married." No ring was presented on bended knee. The scene was more of a business deal, one forged from the heart between two like-minded souls. Katie later admitted, "We had a lot in common, so marriage made sense. We both liked to ski, loved the outdoors, beer, bike rides, and swimming."

That night, Katie went out to the Elkhart Lake taverns and celebrated by herself. Bob went home to bed and set his alarm for an early work hour.

A few days later, Bob drove to Manitowoc, Wisconsin, about 30 minutes north of Sheboygan. He parked his car outside of Rummele's Jewelry Store, went inside, and returned with a wedding ring. He claimed that it "wasn't a big deal," but for Katie, the ring represented the start of a new life.

The Quiet Icon

Bob was pleased with his marriage plan. Everything was succeeding splendidly. The Wigwam Mills president was checking the boxes of this transaction, monitoring its progress, and making forecasts for the future. But to make his engagement official, he needed to ask Katie's father for his permission to marry his daughter. Bob invited his fiancé and her parents to meet him at his apartment.

Bob remembered, "I lived in small apartment above a garage off 6th Street. It was a real bachelor pad, with not much in there, just the basics." Amidst those minimal trappings of single life, James Roenitz blessed Bob's request to have his daughter's hand in marriage. Everyone celebrated over dinner at a local restaurant.

News about Bob and Katie's engagement quickly spread. Bob took calls from friends. Would he like a bachelor party? His pals insisted that the occasion demanded one. They promised booze, taverns, women, and a limo to drive them around town. Bob told them he was too old for a bachelor party, and that he "wanted nothing to do with that foolishness."

On February 26, 1977, James Roenitz walked his daughter Katie down the aisle of St. Clement's Catholic Church in Sheboygan. Bob was 39 years old, and Katie was 33. About one hundred people, mostly family members, stood in the pews. Some dabbed their eyes with handkerchiefs, and most everyone marveled that the "confirmed bachelor" was about to accept a bride.

Katie's sisters, Chris and Ruth, were the bridesmaids, and JoEllen was the maid of honor. They wore billowy, ruffled rust and yellow-colored dresses and wide, matching hats, an outfit that Katie pronounced "weird." Bob's best men were his brother Jim, and Katie's brothers Jim, Tom, and Bob. All sported traditional tuxedos and wide, fat neckties, typical of the 1970s look. Presiding were Bob's Lutheran minister, G. William Genzler, and Katie's Catholic monsignor, Vernon Kuehn.

The reception was held at Pine Hills Country Club, with a sit-down dinner and a live band. In retrospect, both Katie and Bob pronounced their wedding day "uneventful and nothing special." Bob admitted, "We couldn't wait to get out of there." They left the reception at 8:00 p.m., drove to Milwaukee, and then boarded a bus for Chicago. They spent

Newlyweds Katie and Bob Chesebro (left) and Josephine and Robert Roenitz, dance at the wedding reception.

their wedding night at a private club near Lake Michigan, courtesy of Bud Patterson, a salesman who sold yarn to Wigwam.

From Chicago, Katie and Bob flew to Austria for a skiing honeymoon. They checked into their upscale resort and went to the dining hall for dinner. "It was embarrassing," recalled Bob. "Everyone was dressed in tuxedos, and we were in our sweaters." They retreated upstairs and ordered a meal from room service. The next day, Bob bought himself a suit and a formal dress for Katie, which pleased the wait staff.

The skiing was disappointing. Warm weather made sloppy snow, and fog obscured the mountain scenery. After visiting Salzburg and attending a ski show in France, the couple returned to Wisconsin.

Almost immediately, Bob flew to Las Vegas for a sales event. It was a major occasion attended by skiing industry representatives from around the country, making it an ideal venue for showcasing Wigwam Mills products. Sporting his trademark bowtie, Bob staffed the display booth, greeting current and prospective customers. At night, he dined with suppliers and regional sales staff.

Within 72 hours, Bob had transitioned from a European honeymoon to intense business affairs halfway around the world. Exhausted and satiated with Las Vegas food and drink, he became stricken with chest pains. Hhe phoned his cardiologist brother, Jim, who told him to head to a hospital.

Bob checked in and explained his symptoms. The doctors said things could be serious. They sent him to intensive care for three days of testing. When able, Bob phoned his sales staff for show updates. Some visited him at his bedside, and Katie flew to Las Vegas to be with him. Rumors circulated around Sheboygan that Bob Chesebro had a heart attack and might not make it.

The doctor personally delivered the test results. He shut the door, moved a chair next to Bob's hospital bed, and sat down. He shuffled through papers, looked at Bob, and said that everything was normal. The symptoms were probably due to stress and dehydration. The doctor told Bob to "drink more water and get more sleep." He was discharged, and the next day, he flew home to Wisconsin.

Bob still harbored concerns about his health. He drove to see his brother at the Mayo Clinic in Rochester, Minnesota, and underwent many tests. The results were clean and his heart was fine.

Needing a place to live, the newlyweds briefly moved into Chesebro home on Euclid Avenue in Sheboygan. Bob's parents were wintering in Scottsdale, Arizona, so they had the house to themselves. In 1977, the couple bought their first home at 330 Vollrath Boulevard.

The sale was arranged by Katie's mother, who knew the owners. The husband had died, and his widow didn't want to live there alone, so she happily sold the home and all its furnishings. It was a modest one-story, white-painted stucco house with three bedrooms and an attached garage. Bob converted one of the bedrooms into his home office. Proud to be owners of a well-appointed home, Katie and Bob hosted many weekend dinners for friends and family.

Bob admitted, "My social life changed when I married Katie. She had a lot of friends, and they were younger and more active." Hal Peters, a friend and Wigwam sales representative, said, "Marriage completed Bob as an individual, and that benefitted those who worked for him. He now experienced what it meant to be a husband, and the time and responsibilities needed for that."

THE NEXT GENERATION

On December 12, 1977, Bob became a father. Katie gave birth to a daughter they named Margaret; she was an early Christmas present.

When asked what she remembered about the birthing, Katie said, "I was on my back, looking up at the ceiling at St. Nicolas Hospital. There was a really nice light fixture that I thought would look great at the Elkhart Lake cottage." The next day, she asked if she could have it; the hospital staff took it down and gave it to her. The scenario was typical Katie: thinking and doing things that were a bit unordinary.

Two years later, son Christopher was born on May 11, 1979.

Recalling his own father, Bob wanted to be different. He pledged to be more engaged with his children's lives, making Margaret and Chris his priority. When Bob was growing up, Robert Sr. often prioritized Wigwam before family. Robert Sr. was a good man but often distant. Bob's softer heart wouldn't let him be that way.

He mostly succeeded. Bob was scoutmaster of Chris's Boy Scout troop and encouraged him to become an Eagle Scout, the pinnacle of scouting success. Chris recalled, "Dad was always interested in us, and wanted to do things with us. The two of us went on a long canoe trip in the Boundary

The Quiet Icon

Katie and Bob Chesebro Jr. with children Chris and Margaret in 1989.

Waters of Minnesota, and I remember going to sporting goods conventions in Chicago. He was proud of us."

"We grew up humble," Margaret recalled. "Even though we were the 'Wigwam Family,' we didn't have a lot of things. Mom and Dad preferred investing in the business and in the community." Their home on Vollrath Avenue was comfortable, but not opulent. Humility and thriftiness was their style.

The Chesebros lived in a traditional, 1970s family structure. Bob worked, and Katie tended to the house and the kids. During the week, Bob arrived home around 6:00

p.m., and he and Katie enjoyed a couple glasses of La Capilla sherry. At the dinner table, Bob asked his children about their days, offered advice if needed, and then it was bedtime.

Margaret remembered, "After bedtime, Dad always went to work in his basement office. I would tiptoe down hallway, peek around the office door, and try to creep up and scare him. He would laugh and give me a hug. He was very loving."

Margaret added that her father had a "whacky side," which many didn't see. In the morning, Bob awakened his children by rubbing his scruffy cheeks on theirs. Margaret said, "When my friends came over, at first they were afraid of Dad because he can seem kind of gruff. But then he'd smile, crack a joke, and they discovered the magic

Bob liked to have fun, although that characteristic was usually buried beneath the responsibilities of owning and operating a large company.

underneath." Around his family, businessman Bob Chesebro could be his playful self.

In a reflective document, Bob wrote about his children:

> *Although Margaret and her brother Chris at times have skirmishes, they basically enjoy each other's company very much and have spent countless hours playing together. And, when either of them were put in the position of having to defend their actions to their parents, it's amazing how quickly each of them came to the defense of each other. Margaret's love for her brother was probably heightened when he had a bout of spinal meningitis and spent a week in the hospital. She understood that he was very sick at the time and appreciated him all the more when he came home.*

Bob was the undisputed leader of Wigwam Mills, but Katie headed the Chesebro household. Margaret admitted, "Growing up, Mom was the 'ringleader.' She planned most of our activities and vacations, and Dad was always up for whatever she decided." Family holidays included Disney World, a dude ranch in Montana, skiing at Steamboat Springs, and a sailing trip through the British Virgin Islands.

One year, Katie said that the family vacation would be very different. It would be challenging and something that no Chesebro had ever accomplished.

The Next Generation

* * *

Isle Royale National Park is located on one of the most distinctive islands in North America. Situated on the northwest side of Lake Superior, Isle Royale is closer to Canada than the United States. At 49 miles long and nine miles wide, the island's wilderness landscape boasts stunning linear ridges and valleys. The rocks are ancient, formed more than one billion years ago, making them the oldest in the world. Wildlife includes wolf, moose, red fox, otters, beavers, and an assortment of raptors.

In the winter, Isle Royale is uninhabitable by humans. Encircled by frozen water, it's cut off from the world. There are no roads, no towns, and no airport. In summer, ferries shuttle visitors to and from the island via the Michigan Upper Peninsula towns of Houghton or Copper Harbor. The ride is about three hours, and seats are filled with backpackers ready to hike the island's trails and camp. Some will be there for a few days, others for weeks. The trekkers are all ages, but most share the common backpacker "look," dressed in a wool hats, expensive parkas (it can rain a lot in the summer), trendy hiking boots, and backpacks filled with food and gear.

After the ferry docks, the backpackers disembark and scatter into the wilderness. They will be on their own to deal with cooking, hiking, bugs, wind, rain, and preparing shelter at night. Nobody will check on them. There are no rest stops, benches, or supply stores. A journey to Isle Royale National Park can be a lot of work, but the rewards of its wilderness can be immeasurable. It's that kind of place.

The Quiet Icon

In 1992, on a cold winter evening around the dinner table, Katie Chesebro told her family that she wanted to go to Isle Royale. Not just her, but the entire family. It would be their summer family vacation. Margaret, then in eighth grade, and Chris, a seventh grader, asked about hotels and restaurants. Katie said there were none. She showed them brochures with pictures of scenic views, Lake Superior, rock cliffs, and even a moose. Her plan was to hike, camp, and cook their food. The trip would last one full week.

Nobody spoke. Camping for a week didn't seem fun. The kids had slept in tents in the backyard, or at Elkhart Lake, where an indoor bathroom and a warm bed were just steps away. Isle Royale was entirely different.

Bob thought it a grand idea. He was always up for a new adventure, and he embraced the idea in his typical way. If he was going to do something, he would research it, prepare for it, and do it properly. Sloppy planning wouldn't be tolerated.

Bob drove everyone to the REI outfitting store in Milwaukee. They bought sleeping bags, food, a small stove, two sturdy tents, a compass, water bottles, backpacks, hiking boots, and even a rope. Back home, they loaded their new backpacks with books and hiked up and down neighborhood hills to get in shape. Motorists slowed and stared at the sight of four people walking around town with big backpacks.

At night, the family looked at maps and planned a route. They decided to start on the most remote part of the island.

The Next Generation

It was a six-hour drive from Sheboygan to the ferry harbor in Houghton, Michigan. The crossing to the island was foggy and a bit eerie. Mighty Lake Superior, known for sinking many huge ships including the *Edmund Fitzgerald*, was remarkably calm. Chris and Margaret went up on deck and peered over the railing and wondered what awaited them.

Halfway through the crossing, when no land was in sight, a park ranger spoke to the passengers. Dressed in a crisply pressed uniform with a name badge, he took a microphone, welcomed everyone onboard, and gave a short introduction about the island. He showed a video that instructed everyone how to be good campers. *Pack out your trash. Camp only in the designated tent areas. Don't leave food out at night. Use the outhouse facilities. Don't feed wildlife. Finally, when you arrive, please give the park ranger your names, emergency contact information, and your route, just in case.*

The ferry finally docked at the Rock Harbor Visitor Center, the island's main entry point. Most everybody got off except the Chesebro family. Few were traveling on to the island's remote west end. For another hour, the ferry skirted the south shore of the island and finally docked at a place named Windigo. There was nothing there except a pier and a small ranger cabin.

Chris recalled, "When we told people we were starting our hike at the island's far west end, they said, 'Wow, you must be experts.'"

The Quiet Icon

The trail was difficult, with steep, uphill switchbacks, and perilous descents. The path was sometimes difficult to see. And then it rained.

Chris recalled, "We just broke camp, and the skies opened up and it was a deluge." The trail got muddy, and the mosquitos were thick. Margaret said, "At that point, everybody cried. We weren't having much fun."

Moods improved with sunshine. Chris went swimming in a lake and emerged covered with tiny black leeches. The overviews of Lake Superior were spectacular, even better than the photos in the brochures. They came face to face with a moose, just several yards away. At night, the stars were like little spotlights. All agreed that never had they shined so brightly. Someone thought they saw a satellite, moving slowly from west to east.

Bob, who was perpetually clean shaven, began growing a beard. Nobody, even his own family, had ever seen him with heavy whiskers. Some wondered whether he could even grow a beard. Three days into the hike, a blanket of blond hairs covered his face. It was the first time he ever looked like an outdoorsman instead of a clean-cut corporate executive.

Eventually he said, "I can't take this anymore," and pulled a small, battery-powered razor from his backpack. Soon he looked like his old self, smooth-faced and ready for the office.

After a week, the family had traversed 49 miles. Margaret recalled, "At the finish, Mom saw a guy with a six-pack of beer and offered him $40 for it. All of us drank it, as sort of a celebration. We needed it."

The Next Generation

A week long camping trip on Lake Superior's Isle Royale National Park was a formative episode in the life of the Chesebro Family. From left to right: Katie, Chris, Margaret, and Bob.

Chris recalled, "The trip to Isle Royale was one of my most remarkable life memories. We didn't know it at the time, but Mom had been diagnosed with multiple myeloma. Back then, that type of cancer could be a death sentence. She wanted the family together on that island for a lifetime experience that we'd never forget."

It worked. The challenging backpacking adventure reinforced the love within the Chesebro family. Although Katie's medical condition often depleted her strength, Margaret, just 12 years old, encouraged her. Katie recalled, "Margaret would tell me, 'Come on, Mom, you can do it!'"

Katie also said that the experience made Chris "grow from a boy into a man."

It was a life-changing journey that wouldn't have happened on a typical vacation. Katie had known that way back in February.

* * *

For all of their similarities, Katie and Bob had different religions.

On Sundays, the Chesebro family worshiped at St. Clements Catholic Church, and Bob took communion, even though he was a baptized and confirmed Lutheran. He recalled, "Some people thought that was a big deal, but I didn't. The Catholic and Lutheran liturgies are very similar, so I was comfortable in the Catholic Church."

One spring day on Chicago's Michigan Avenue, Chris asked his father why he wasn't Catholic. It was a lofty question from a 10-year-old boy, but his mother had put him up to it.

Bob saw no reason to convert to his wife's religion. Neither Katie nor the St. Clement's priest ever suggested it. But Chris's question eventually spurned him to come into full communion with the Catholic Church.

Bob enrolled in the Rite of Christian Initiation of Adults (RCIA), a process through which people become Catholic. On Sundays, he attended an RCIA program led by fellow parishioner Jackie Gruenke. Laid-back and fun, Gruenke guided spirited discussions about the Bible and Catholic teachings and practices. Within a couple of months, Bob became a fully initiated member of the Catholic Church. There was no special ceremony, no announcement, and no baptism.

"It was really pretty easy," remembered Bob. "Katie was Catholic, so I already knew a lot about what was taught. It was more of a formality than an education for me."

Were it not for his son's inquiry in Chicago, Bob might have remained Lutheran. The conversion didn't change Bob's spiritual life, but at least he could now say he was Catholic in the purest sense. No longer did he need to masquerade.

CHIEF BOB

Until his marriage in 1977, Bob's sole focus—his entire life, for that matter—had been devoted to Wigwam Mills. Now he had a wife and a family.

Bob's marriage and children didn't change his business commitments. He just spent more time working at home, and maybe got less sleep. If anything, having a wife and kids motivated him even more. He wanted the best for them and hoped he would make them proud.

In the same year of his marriage, the Sporting Goods Hall of Fame inducted Robert Sr., citing his "profound leadership, innovation, and brand promotion within the sporting goods industry that kept Wigwam in the top of the market." His induction added more credibility to Wigwam's reputation as an industry trailblazer.

Meanwhile, Bob was pioneering his own new territory. An avid skier, he knew the importance of warm feet and head. He expanded the sporting goods market, especially hats, and bolstered Wigwam's line of athletic and outdoor socks.

Bob also had a knack for knowing what would sell and developing new products to fit his hunch. He even named his creations. The Kitzbuhl was his new, heavy-weight ski sock. The Sirocco™ sock combined warmth and comfort. The

The Quiet Icon

Solaris™ was a new silk under sock. The marketing department created images for each name, and many became hot sellers.

Bob's most popular sock was the Moraine. It was a heavy-gauge, wool and cotton sock that was immensely popular in the 1990s. All over America, especially on college campuses, it was trendy to wear socks and sandals. The Moraine was one of the largest selling styles in Wigwam history, and more than 1 million pairs were sold. It was so successful that competitors introduced their own version of the style.

All these Wigwam products benefited from Wigwam's reputation for quality. There was no other sock like it.

Robert E. Chesebro Jr, left, and his father, Robert E. Chesebro Sr., check the quality of a sock in the knitting department of the Wigwam Mills manufacturing plant in Sheboygan. In 1983, when this photo was taken, Bob was CEO and his father was chairman of the board.

Satisfied customers told their friends and neighbors, and retail outlets sold out quickly.

No matter how popular they are, Wigwam socks can't sell themselves. A brochure or catalogue helps, but only a person showing samples can convince a retail buyer to purchase large quantities. The Wigwam sales process is a highly orchestrated and nationwide operation. Only the best people are entrusted to represent the brand and they need to know everything about Wigwam products, down to the yarns and the final construction. They also must possess the "Wigwam personality," being naturally down-to-earth, friendly, and humble. They are the face of not only Wigwam products, but generations of the Chesebro Family.

In the beginning, Hand Knit Hosiery and Wigwam products were sold by the company officers and a national sales force. Robert Sr. traveled the country making calls and hauling suitcases packed with samples. Bob also sold products during his initial years with Wigwam. Trips could last up to three weeks in the larger territories.

Sales associates, employed by agencies, also sold Wigwam items, as well as non-competing goods from other manufacturers. Some agencies have represented Wigwam for generations. Fathers, sons, and even grandsons have "carried the line" in their respective regions. No matter the place, the sales pitch was the same: Wigwam is a family business; everything is knitted domestically, and the products are never the cheapest but are the best quality out there. Being premium has a price.

Bob knew that the best product in the world wouldn't sell if nobody knew about them. The sales force was critical.

The Quiet Icon

Bob regularly picked up the phone to speak to his salespeople and consulted with them at trade shows and sales meetings. He valued their input from product ideas, retail account information, to assessing the overall business climate within their respective areas. He was obsessed with gathering field intelligence to help make informed brand decisions.

Sales conversations could last for hours. Bob's curiosity was boundless, and he always needed to know more. What are the obstacles? Who is buying? What's the best seller? Even then, a salesman's phone might ring the next morning with Bob saying that, overnight, he thought about something and needed an answer.

One salesman, Don Mezsaros, was the CEO of a sales company founded by his father. The firm had sold the Wigwam line for more than 45 years. Mezsaros recalled, "When I was younger, and just starting out, I'd go to the Wigwam sales meetings. I was only 28 years old and all the other sales guys were seasoned sales veterans, but Bob wanted me there. He saw something in me and was willing to give me a chance. He wanted my opinion. That meant a lot to me. Bob was a very thoughtful, kind man."

Another sales representative, Jim Einhauser, met Bob in the early 1980s when he was working as a buyer for American Eagle Outfitters. Wigwam supplied socks to American Eagle, and Einhauser immediately sensed that the company was different. Many manufacturers had a revolving door of leaders and sold products of inconsistent quality. Some even practiced questionable ethics. At Wigwam, Einhauser saw the opposite: integrity, a passion for quality, and leaders who honored business partnerships.

Chief Bob

In 1994, Bob hired Einhauser as executive vice-president of marketing and sales. On his first day, Einhauser saw an envelope with his name on it. Inside were knitting machine needles of varying sizes. Right then, he knew that the Wigwam knitting process was tremendously important.

Einhauser remembered, "Bob told me if you're going to sell for Wigwam, you need to learn everything about knitting. You need to know the best yarns or combination of yarns for each product. You must understand how each knitting machine operates, and what machines make each item. Wigwam knits better than anyone else, and you darn well better understand why."

It was an intimidating way to begin a job, but Einhauser respected Bob's passion for making exceptional knitwear.

Wigwam salesmen needed to demonstrate impeccable personal and professional qualities, and also have passion. Just showing up for a commission check wasn't acceptable. Salesmen had to be there because they loved knitting and wanted to represent a great product.

Before his first sales call, Bob insisted that Einhauser work in every department of the plant to see each distinctive manufacturing process. This also immersed him into the Wigwam company culture. Wigwam workers were loyal and happy, and Einhauser needed to fit in. It was a workplace where employees knew about each other's families, hobbies, and how they spent their weekends. Selling for that type of manufacturer wasn't for everyone.

The Quiet Icon

Einhauser and Bob often spent 16 hours a day together. There was airplane travel, trade shows, industry events, and board, and staff meetings. The two would pass each other in the hallway, and a brief "hello" could morph into an hour-long hallway conversation about products and sales. Their opinions sometimes differed. They argued. They raised their voices. But at the end of the day, they chuckled about it and moved forward.

Bob became the most influential mentor in Einhauser's life. Einhauser admitted, "Not only did I look to him as a leader, but he was also a father figure. I never told him that directly, but he knew." Bob called Einhauser "our best sales

Jim Einhauser, vice-president of sales and marketing, is pictured at a Wigwam Mills retail store. Bob said, "Einhauser was our best sales guy."

and marketing guy." It was an impeccable match of talents and personalities.

Bob was adamant that his salespeople—and everyone else, for that matter—knew that Wigwam knitted and didn't weave. There is a big difference. Knitting is a series of interconnected loops, and weaving crosses the fibers over each other. Knitted fabric is more elastic, and woven fabric can only be stretched one way. It's more complicated than that, and Bob could explain differences using terms that only experts understood. Even then, some of the pros were flummoxed. Bob was a knitting nerd who knew more than necessary, but he couldn't help himself. Knitting was his life and his favorite company department.

Bob was also a master of yarns. He was proficient in sizes, fibers, spinning methods, finishing techniques, and tensile strengths. For visual and technical reasons, several Wigwam socks had five or six different yarns knit into them. Yarn salesmen had to be ready because Bob often knew more about their product than they did. The unprepared, or those with an inferior product, were politely shown the door.

Yarns are multifaceted, and the machines that knit yarn are a whirl of complexity. Gone were the days of the Hand Knit Hosiery Company and images of grandmothers knitting in rocking chairs. Today, sophisticated automation does the work, and Bob knew everything about the latest knitting technologies including needles, cylinders, motors, and the process of reciprocation.

In the 1980s, Bob travelled to Europe to explore some of the continent's modern knitting automations. The Europeans were ahead of the USA in this regard, and Bob was

The Quiet Icon

intrigued. He finally discovered a unique knitting machine in Italy, one unlike any other he had seen. Manufactured by the Moreni Machine Company, the machine could automatically make the important rib stitch with two needles instead of just one. No other machine had this ability and Bob was smitten.

The machines were expensive, but Bob purchased some anyway and shipped them to the Wigwam plant. After installation, they began making the Moraine, the immensely popular wool sock. The new Italian machines helped Wigwam churn out more than 60,000 pairs of these thick socks each day. It was a manufacturing miracle. The demand for ragg wool socks was so high that a third shift was added, and manufacturing became a 24-hour-a-day operation. The Moreni machine made it all possible.

It also gave Bob an excuse to travel to Italy, his favorite European nation. He loved the food, the wine, and the classic Italian hospitality shown to him by the executives of the Moreni Machine Company. He was one of their best customers.[12]

There were other investments. Bob had solar panels installed to heat water. He studied technology and computers. Even in the 1970s, when computers were huge, complex machines that could occupy an entire room, Bob wanted to

---

[12] As a gift, the Moreni Machine Company shipped Bob a battery-powered, stand-up scooter. Named the "Biga," it had handlebars, a horn, and a light. Its top speed was about 5 mph. Bob drove it around the factory, but sometimes crashed into things. According to long-time employee Susan Kettler, "Somebody finally took the keys away from Bob because he was not a good scooter driver."

know how they could help. According to Don Mezaros, "Bob wasn't afraid of technology. He was willing to use computers for business forecasting, inventory management, and financials." Dave Fischer, the former manager of Wigwam plant operations, added, "If there was anything new in manufacturing, Bob led the way, especially with computers."

While many businesses remained skeptical about computers, Bob assembled a Technical Information department (IT) and hired a consultant to implement companywide computerization. Within a couple of weeks, the group handed Bob a thick, spiral-bound book with their recommendations. There was a lot of technical jargon, and Bob asked questions. If Wigwam was going to spend inordinate sums of money on computers, he wanted to know everything he could about them, and how they would help.

Soon, IBM computers were in nearly every department. The staff was trained to use them, and the machines did many of the calculations that had been done by hand. After the initial learning curve, and a lot of trial and error, life got easier for many employees. A computer was just faster, smarter, and more efficient than the old ways of doing things. Bob recalled, "I pushed the idea of having a system that we could use to run the business, especially a forecasting program that could predict sales by size, color, and style."

The changeover was so successful that people from the IBM marketing staff came to Wigwam to make a promotional video. They filmed for three days and produced a video showing the proper use and implementation of their IBM software. Bob had a starring role.

The Quiet Icon

Margaret said, "Dad was very different from his father. He always embraced change within the company."

Through all of this, Robert Sr. was ailing. The former dynamic leader of Wigwam Mills was frail, succumbing to the effects of two strokes and old age. He died in a local nursing home on October 9, 1992. Bob was at his bedside. "That was hard for me. Dad's funeral was secondary to the shock of seeing him wither away. It was painful." Robert Chesebro Sr. was 89 years old.

* * *

For a long time, Sheboygan was one of those towns where people did the same thing—every day. They lived in one house, went on the same vacation, and ate at the same restaurant. Change and variety were not a part of their lives. Being predictable was just more comfortable.

That's mostly changed, except in the workplace. In Sheboygan County, it's still common for employees to retire after 50 years with the same company. That's the Sheboygan way because there are a lot of employers that are just too good to leave. Wigwam Mills is one of them. The average tenure of a Wigwam worker is 17 years, and many have been there for their entire working lives.

Bob knew that employee loyalty was the core of his success, and without them, there would be no socks, hats, scarves or anything else with the Wigwam label. Nor would anybody be talking about what a great place Wigwam was to work. Bob sent handwritten notes to his people when they needed a bit of encouragement, condolences, or gratitude. An employee might receive a note from the boss, with the opening "I just heard that your daughter got married.

Congratulations!" He often closed with, "thanks for being a part of the Wigwam Family." He would write whether he knew the person personally or not. Bob even penned notes to workers on their employment date anniversary.

Bob viewed his office, with desk, credenza, and shelves packed so full of paperwork that they often collapsed, as a business necessity. But every weekday, and sometimes more often, he visited the manufacturing floor. When he entered, the entire energy of the place changed. People perked up, smiled, and wanted to greet him, even if it was just to say hello. Bob was genuinely curious about their well-being. He asked questions, and many offered suggestions about how to improve things. Bob had remarkable camaraderie with his

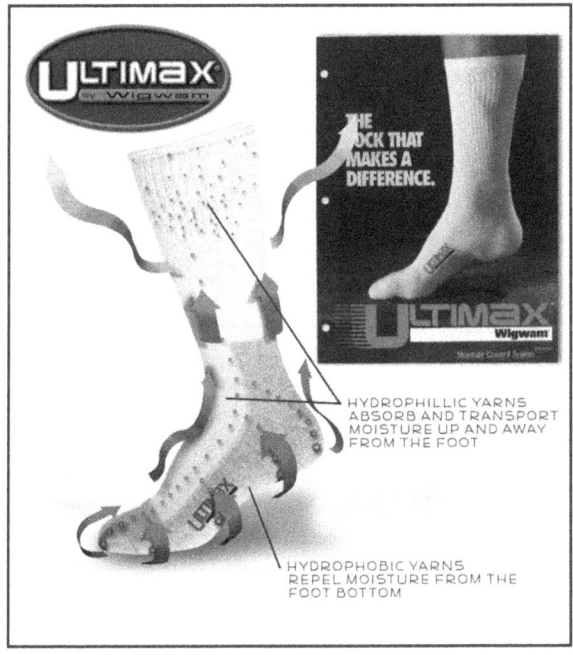

people; it didn't matter if you were a company executive, or part of the cleaning staff. Everyone was treated like the most important person in the room.

Einhauser said, "Bob was direct, fair, thoughtful, extremely analytical, stern, insightful, and quite humorous. He gave people a sense of place and a sense of accomplishment. He had a laser focus on the big picture, and distinct ability to understand all the moving parts of making a business successful. For most employees, every day was an opportunity to learn something new and useful from Bob that would help keep Wigwam a force within the industry."

In a way, Bob made himself into his father's antithesis. Whereas his father could be indifferent toward people, Bob often measured himself by his image in the minds of others. It was sometimes a preoccupation, verging on obsession that would guide his energies. By instinct or by study, he had an exceptionally firm grasp of human beings and how to appeal to them. He put himself in other people's shoes.

Bob was particularly empathetic to the local Hmong population, whose ancestors were peaceful hill county farmers in northeastern Laos. The Hmong didn't immigrate to America voluntarily. Their story is a little-known episode of wartime horrors.

During the Vietnam War, the North Vietnamese launched an offensive into the Hmong homeland. With the help of the CIA, the Hmong fought back, but Laos eventually fell to the communists in 1975. Seeking freedom, many Hmong left on foot for Thailand, a long and arduous journey through thick and uninhabited forests. Along the way, they endured constant threat of Communist capture, or more likely, being shot and killed. Those who survived spent years in Thai refugee camps. Many were eventually resettled in Wisconsin.

Bob found the Hmong to be smart, capable, and reliable workers. He hired many, and in his office hangs a Hmong tapestry depicting their heroic escape from their occupied homeland, presented to him by his Hmong employees.

Bob believed that there was a direct correlation between happy employees and a clean and comfortable working environment. Every department boss was required to keep their areas in perfect working order. Einhauser remembered, "I gave countless tours to a wide variety of groups and individuals. They always mentioned how clean and modern the facility was."

All of the Chesebro leaders valued good employee relations. They knew that it wasn't enough to pay well and have good working conditions. People needed to be recognized and appreciated. A hearty "thank you" was always welcome, but over time, that became less special. Sometimes a bigger and better show of gratitude was necessary.

Knowing this, Robert Sr. began the Wigwam 25 Year Club to honor employees who had worked there that long. Bob continued the tradition. There is a banquet, speeches, and a lot of fun. Some years, as many as 20 people received their quarter-century plaque or a gold watch.

At recent events, Bob was the master of ceremonies. He was always entertaining, witty, and presented the awards. The 25-Year Club honorees then spoke about how they were grateful for the opportunity, and thanked Bob and his family. They told stories about how Wigwam hired them

The Quiet Icon

when they needed a part-time job so they could earn extra money. Twenty-five years later, they were still there. Some began working there when Robert Sr. was still president.

In 1958, at age 20, Dave Fischer began working for Bob's father. He was paid $1.00 an hour, and a year later, he was promoted to "washer" at $1.35 an hour. Around age 30, he wanted to finish his college degree in economics. At that time, Bob was president and supported Fischer's goals. He told him, "You may be in college, but I want you to come into the plant every week and make sure that our new sock dryer is performing well." Only Fischer could make that assessment. The arrangement worked, and after graduation, Fischer eventually became manager of plant operations, overseeing 400 people and the manufacturing process. He retired in 2003 after 44 years.

Stories like Fischer's are common. Many begin by saying "Wigwam believed in me and gave me a chance." Others credit Bob Chesebro for their devotion. In the end, it didn't matter whether it was Wigwam or Bob who received praise. The two names were synonymous.

* * *

Several times a year, the executive staff hosted an employee "lunch" for all three shifts of the plant and the office personnel. A buffet was set up in the plant cafeteria, and the bosses served each employee as they went through the line.

This was not a simple process. The event required nearly 24 hours of preparation, service, and clean-up. The third-shift employees were served lunch at 5:45 a.m. before

Chief Bob

they went home. At noon, the first shift and the office staff were served. At 10:00 p.m., the second shift had plates in hand, accepting food served by the Wigwam brass.

Bob also made sure that his employees knew how the company was performing. Quarterly employee meetings, held by shift, were hosted in the break room. Armed with an overhead projector, and later with PowerPoint, Bob shared both good and bad news. Reports such as financial, sales, and marketing information were laid bare. Questions were asked, and Bob patiently answered. There were no secrets at Wigwam, and rumors rarely circulated. Everyone knew what was going on. Bob said, "We were always as honest and open with them as we could be." At the end of the meeting, Bob reminded everybody to take advantage of the company's profit-sharing program. Wigwam matched contributions, and worker participation was exceptionally high.

Bob had established himself as a capable company boss. But he, too, had superiors. The Wigwam Mills board of directors gathered quarterly and listened to many reports. In these meetings, Bob was clear-cut and straightforward. Information was delivered and decisions made. Director Richard Pauls remembered, "Overall, the company was usually in good shape. But it wasn't colorful. Nobody wasted a dime on amenities. We didn't even have a board meeting room. We'd meet in an office without snacks, coffee, or water." Pauls eventually pulled Bob aside and said, "Bob, can we at least have some water when we get together?" At the next board meeting, there was one bottle of water for each director.

The Quiet Icon

* * *

Since nearly the dawn of the Industrial Age, employees have gone on strike. Photos of angry workers holding picket signs make the front-page news. Reporters write stories about closed production lines, stressed families, and frayed relations. A drawn-out, knock 'm down strike might make good headlines, but it has repercussions. Some companies and people never fully recover.

The employees of Wigwam Mills never went on strike. Just the thought of it was anathema. Wigwam was a happy place. Workers and management had kids in the same schools, went to the same events, and shopped at the same stores. Many were good friends, and even related. Walking out on a company that truly cared about you just didn't seem right.

Many Wigwam personnel were members of the Textile Workers Union. Bob recalled, "The textiles union was difficult. I met with the president often and became disenchanted with the union's attitude. Its leadership was male dominated and from out-of-state, and their goal seemed to be to foster disenchantment with our workers."

In the 1990s, Wigwam employees decided to strike. They made picket signs after work and met on weekends to plan their tactics. Dave Fischer recalled, "It seems odd now, but the employees wanted a $100 annual benefit for personal emergencies. The company was against it. Eventually, we caved and came to our senses. It wasn't worth going on strike for a $100-year benefit."

Wigwam workers knew they had a good thing going. Friends who worked for other companies often complained about their jobs, their bosses, their pay. You almost never heard that from Wigwam personnel.

That contentment stemmed from Wigwam's history of treating people well. The company archives, stored in old file cabinets and stacked on shelves, have more than 100 years' worth of product catalogues, photographs, and documents. There's enough memorabilia for a museum.

Jim Einhauser paged through a 1910 catalogue and saw the same family pride and quality that Bob still demanded. He explained, "The brand means everything to Bob. He doesn't see just socks. He sees his father and his grandfather and the family legacy. I was just one of many passing through the halls, but Bob and his ancestors have been there for their lifetimes."

Those ancestors began current Wigwam partnerships even before Bob was born. Crescent Woolen Mills, located north of Sheboygan, was founded by the Webster family in 1867. Archibald and Theodore Webster began supplying woolen spun yarn to Bob's grandfather in 1923. Crescent and Wigwam are remarkably similar, or as Bob would say, "Their philosophy of business is the same, except they manufacture yarn, and we manufacture socks."

For more than a century, Wigwam and Crescent grew up arm in arm. Both survived the growing pains of changing marketplaces and economic downturns. Each company operates in a small town and is managed by descendants of the founders. Both had employees who would never consider working anywhere else.

Bob always went out of his way to support Guy Webster. Guy was remarkably responsive to Wigwam's needs, and Crescent Woolen Mills always provided a quality product. Like the Chesebros, the Webster family did business ethically and honestly. Handshake agreements were enough.

Bud Patterson was another long-standing business partner. Patterson began selling yarn to Bob's father in the 1930s. When he was in his 80s, Patterson still drove six hours round trip from his Chicago home to sell yarn to Bob Jr. Born in an era when airplanes were still considered a dangerous novelty, Patterson looked like he'd stepped off the screen of a 1940s black and white film noir movie. He dressed impeccably, appearing in shined shoes and a black suit with a white handkerchief peeking from the breast pocket. Even his car was black, and his license plate read YARNS. Patterson spoke with an almost theatrical lilt and was a consummate gentleman.

Patterson witnessed four decades of Wigwam's evolution and appreciated its success story. He was a wizard of yarns, and Bob highly respected him. He matched Bob's knowledge of product intricacies, and the two men could spend hours talking about yarn fibers, sizes, and plies, using terms that only yarn aficionados could understand. Patterson always requested a morning meeting so that he could host everyone to lunch afterward. Bud Patterson was like the fun uncle who everyone wanted to be around.

Bud Patterson and the Webster family are emblematic of the long-standing business relationships forged and stewarded by Wigwam. Bob understood that business relationships were almost like having multiple children; for them to flourish, everyone needed personal attention. Collaboration meant friendships, trust, and maybe even a dose of love. "It's also the way we like to do things in Sheboygan," Bob explained. He detested slick sales hucksters who toted excessive paperwork, legal contracts, and had limited passion for the industry.[13]

Personal attention required travel, and Bob was often away from home. He was living the Chinese proverb that says, "Do what you love, and you'll never work a day in your life." Katie often pleaded for Bob to take time off, but there was always another convention, trade show, or meeting.

Even sports weren't a deterrent from work. Bob followed the Green Bay Packers because it was the most talked about topic in Wisconsin during football season. Professional basketball and baseball didn't interest him whatsoever. In summer, he played golf, biked, and swam.

When Bob was away in Italy, the Wigwam marketing department decided that Katie needed her husband at home. The staff created a life-size, cardboard cutout of Bob, and snuck it into the breezeway of the Chesebro house. Days later, Katie sent pictures of "Bob" and her at the beach, driving around town, and having a meal together.

Everyone chuckled about "Cardboard Bob," but they also appreciated that Bob preferred a personal connection in an era of text messaging and emails. That took him away from home, but it was worth it.

---

[13] Bud Patterson passed away in 2022. Crescent Woolen Mills was sold in 2014, but the Webster family remains involved in its operations.

The Quiet Icon

* * *

In 2005, Wigwam Mills celebrated its 100th anniversary. One of the events was held at the original manufacturing facility on 1321 N. 14th Street. Once-upon-a-time, the name Hand Knit Hosiery Company was painted on the outside bricks. Sixty years later, it was a brewery.

Bob had not been inside that building for decades. Jim Einhauser asked the brewery owner if they could visit the non-renovated parts of the facility. They stepped over construction materials, broken glass, and piles of dirt. In one hallway, Bob opened the glass-windowed door to his father's former office. It was a mess, but much remained as Bob remembered it. He gently touched his father's desk and blew dust off the shelves. In the corner, the same coat rack was still there. It was 2005, but Bob was transported back to 1960, when he was 22 years old.

The pinnacle of the 100th anniversary was an open house held at the Wigwam plant on Crocker Avenue. Attending were Sheboygan dignitaries, business and government leaders, employees, retirees, friends, and other VIPs including Herbert Kohler, CEO of the Kohler Company, and the Wisconsin governor. The place was decorated with balloons, streamers, and historic photos. A story about the anniversary made the front page of the next morning's newspaper.

Bob was the most popular man in the room. People crowded around and shook his hand. Many hugged him. He posed for photographs and gave short interviews. When it was time to speak, he strode to the podium, sharply dressed in a suit with a lapel carnation and a colorful bowtie. He cleared his throat, shuffled his notes, and scanned the room. He saw people he loved, and he knew they loved him back. He saw grandparents hired by his father, their children and grandchildren, all of whom had worked for Wigwam. During his remarks he reflected on what everyone meant to him. He was introspective, thankful, funny, and humble.

It was a proud moment. The boy who was a "late bloomer" had successfully guided the family company into its 100th year. Rarely does a third-generation family business survive for a century. It was a monumental achievement, and although the Hand Knit Hosiery Company had changed dramatically with the times, a Chesebro was still the company leader. Bob's grandfather's dream was alive and prospering. Einhauser said, "Robert was in total control over Wigwam's direction."

John Wilder added, "I was amazed at Bob's ability to fit his company into the mainstream of sock production despite intense foreign competition. He was exceptionally clever to capture the market and keep Wigwam viable."

* * *

Amidst all this, Bob's mother, Helen Prange Chesebro, turned 100 years old in July 2002. At her bedside were cake and balloons, and family members sang *Happy Birthday*. Still living at home on Euclid Avenue in Sheboygan, Bob transformed the living room into her bedroom, and hired live-in caretakers. She was nearly blind and suffered from mild dementia.

Six months later, Helen died in a hospital and Bob was with her. A memorial service was held at the First United Lutheran Church. She was buried at Wildwood Cemetery on

The Quiet Icon

a cold, blustery January day. As she was laid to rest, Bob remembered his youth, when he was awkward and shy, and how his mother was always reassuring and supportive. His father knew business, but his mother understood people. She had a way of making everyone happy and content. Helen Prange Chesebro gave him strength when he needed it most. Now that pillar in his life was gone.

DUTY AND OBLIGATION

Bob valued traditions and legacies. This was especially true with charity, where many of his chosen causes had been supported by his father and grandfather. As a Chesebro, he was duty-bound to help charities that his ancestors found worthy. One of these was the Rotary Club.

Bob's grandfather was among the first Wisconsin Rotarians. Founded in 1905, the Rotary Club was a way for professionals with diverse backgrounds to exchange ideas and form lifelong friendships. Over time, Rotary's mission extended to humanitarian service and charity.

Robert Sr. was a Rotarian, and Bob eventually joined in the mid-1960s. At first, he sat quietly in the background, overshadowed by his popular and outspoken father. Later, when his father began ailing, young Bob spoke up, volunteered, and led. He assisted fundraising efforts for various projects and was named head of Sheboygan Rotary Foundation.

Forty years later, in 2012, Bob Chesebro was presented with the prestigious Rotary Good Citizenship Award. the highest Rotary honor, given to extraordinarily philanthropic citizens. Previous winners were Sheboygan's industry and philanthropic leaders, including both Herb and Terry Kohler.

The Quiet Icon

The criteria for the award reads, in part:

> *The candidate must have an exemplary record as a citizen; be loyal to our country, its ideals and institutions; and perform civic duties efficiently and well. He/she has taken an active part in the life of the community and in making Sheboygan County a desirable place to live. Keeping well-informed concerning community affairs, he/she has given freely of time and energy to advance community interests. The candidate must be of good character and exemplify high standards and ethics.*

Bob accepted the award at a banquet held at the Sheboygan Yacht Club. After the dinner, Bob spoke. He told the crowd that being philanthropic was part of living a responsible adult life. If you had a job, a place to live, and food on your table, you should help others. The expression "to whom much is given, much is expected" should be a life guidepost for those who were blessed.

He spoke about his ancestors, all of whom were charitable in heart and in service. Charity was simply the right thing to do, always. The health of a community is important. Receiving the award was meaningful, but others deserved recognition as well. Fundraising was a team effort. He couldn't have done it alone.

When the standing ovation concluded, Bob took his seat and wondered what all the fuss was about. He was just doing what was expected of him, guided by his heart. There was nothing more to it.

Bob encouraged everyone, especially his Wigwam employees, to be community stewards. Jon Doll, former executive director of the United Way of Sheboygan County, said that Wigwam Mills was one of the few companies that allowed him to speak directly with the workers about the importance of giving. "Most companies just wrote a check. But Bob wanted his people to hear firsthand how United Way was helping those in need."

Whether he intended it or not, Bob had become a highly regarded fundraiser and nonprofit volunteer. Many nonprofit executives asked Bob to serve on their board of directors. They knew he'd raise money and get things done. He accepted some requests and turned down many.

Bob found nonprofit board meetings frustrating. Coming from a corporate lineage, where decisions were made and quickly enacted, Bob lamented the slow-moving, nonprofit ways. Most everything had to be evaluated, researched, approved by committees, then endlessly discussed at meetings, and even reviewed with constituents. Everything took too much time.

As a result, Bob could be outspoken and impatient. At the end of meetings, colleagues might remind him, "Bob, this isn't your company. You need to be more tolerant. There is no king in a charity. Everyone gets a say."

It's not that Bob was uncooperative and only wanted his way. He was simply accustomed to achieving results quickly.

The Quiet Icon

He eventually tempered his expectations, realizing the cause was most important. If the road to success had detours, so be it.

One of those charitable roads led him to the Sheboygan YMCA.

* * *

In 1844, George Williams founded the YMCA in London, England. The city known today as an attractive and vibrant place was very different then. Although London was the capital of the largest empire in the world, it was notoriously filthy. The air was thick with choking, sooty fog, and human sewage floated down the Thames River. Thievery was rampant. The streets were filled with mud and horse manure. In summertime, flies clustered on everything both indoors and outside. Millions of people lived in poverty and disease and plague were common. The YMCA was started, in part, to create a supportive community to help young men deal with the challenges of existing in this rough environment.

Seven years later, around the beginning of the American Civil War, the first American YMCA opened in Boston's Old South Church on Boylston Street. For men needing help, especially fresh immigrants, the YMCA offered mentoring, athletics, hot meals, and boarding rooms. The YMCA was an oasis for those who desired fellowship and friendships. The concept rapidly spread across the nation.

The Sheboygan YMCA began in the 1890s. It was initially a two-room affair above a bank building on downtown 8th Street before it moved to a larger building down the road. The new location featured Sheboygan's first bowling alleys, meeting rooms, and a lunch counter. In 1902, the location was abandoned due to lack of funds. The "Y" was eventually resurrected, but closed during the Great Depression.

Sometime in the late 1930s, Bob's father joined the Sheboygan YMCA and was later elected to the board of directors. In 1944, Robert Sr. and his fellow directors decided that a new building was needed. They planned for a sparkling new facility near Lake Michigan, one so stunning that men would clamor for membership.

Fundraising began. In four years, the community pledged $428,000[14] for the new YMCA. Robert Sr. personally raised much of it, admitting that the YMCA was one of his favorite charitable causes. He believed in the pursuit of health and wellness, and that everyone, regardless of income, should be able to enjoy the Y. The new building was completed in 1956 and was one of the most comprehensive YMCA facilities in the Great Lakes region. The dedication was, as one dignitary put it, "a spectacle of splendor fitting for the fine city of Sheboygan."

Like many nonprofits, the Sheboygan YMCA was in continual fundraising mode. As soon as the dedication ribbons were cut in 1956, the YMCA staff and board were planning new projects. That mindset was necessary to keep the YMCA viable. In the nonprofit sector, you are either fundraising or withering.

---

[14] About $3.4 million at the time of this book's publication.

The Quiet Icon

When Bob joined the Sheboygan YMCA board of directors, he knew he would have to raise money. Not just a few dollars, but millions.

Most people don't like asking others for money. For Bob, it came naturally, and he enjoyed the process. It gave him a reason to invite business friends for lunch or dinner. At some point during the meal, Bob made certain the prospect knew that Katie and he had generously pledged a gift to the local Y. It was his way of saying, "if we believe in this, so should you."

In 1973, Bob accepted his first fundraising challenge. The YMCA needed a new gymnasium, an Olympic-size pool, and a locker room renovation. The goal was $500,000,[15] and Bob was appointed chairman of the Business and Industry Division, which made him the leader of securing donations from his corporate peers. The campaign nearly doubled its goal by raising nearly $1 million.

At the dedication gala, Bob shook hands, gave a short address, and was robustly congratulated. It was a noteworthy fundraising accomplishment for a 35-year-old young man.

His success brought more YMCA assignments. Between 1984 and 2013, Bob orchestrated three additional fund campaigns, which together raised almost $12 million. The projects included funds for a new YMCA branch in nearby Sheboygan Falls, a new weight and aerobic room, childcare center, and improvements to the summer camp, Camp Y-Koda. In each instance, Bob and Katie gave generously.

---

[15] About $2.1 million at the time of this book's publication.

Duty and Obligation

Some claimed Bob was the most dedicated volunteer in the history of the Sheboygan YMCA.

Executive Director Donna Wendlandt, explained Bob's magic. "Bob will speak with almost anyone about anything. He's very non-judgmental and quite engaging." This made Bob a natural fundraiser. He'd meet with a donor prospect, explain the need, and always emerge with a sizeable gift pledge. Around town, it was known that if Bob Chesebro invited you for a meal, you might be asked for money. Even so, people joined him. He had a magnetism that was hard to refuse. His friend Eleanor Jung said, "Bob is the nicest person I know."

Bob knew exactly what people and businesses to call on. His mind held a Rolodex of donors, many of whom he knew personally. He assembled a fundraising team to help him. He told them what to say, how to say it, how much to ask for, and followed up with his people to make sure they performed.

Some fell short of his expectations. If Bob deemed a gift pledge "too low," he'd take the donor to lunch himself. When the bill arrived, the donor had doubled their gift pledge, and maybe even given Bob the key to their vacation home. His charm and persuasive tactics were always at championship level.

In 2011, Katie and Bob Chesebro were given the YMCAs Lifetime Service Award. The plaque recognizes both dedication and decades of service on behalf of the Y.

Since the time of Bob's grandfather, the YMCA had morphed into something larger and more diverse than its founders imagined. The Young Men's Christian Association

The Quiet Icon

is now identified with daycare, swimming pools, exercise rooms, tennis, summer camps, and wellness seminars, and Bob appreciated its broad service to many diverse groups. Besides the YMCA, another local organization was equally as impactful in its own intimate way and Bob sometimes became emotional when talking about it.

* * *

Some jobs are a calling. Those who devote their lives to helping others know what this means. They choose work that requires long hours and patience. The pay is often low, but to these caretakers, it doesn't matter. Their life mission is to help, aid, and heal.

Caretakers don't view themselves as divinity. They'll tell you that they are merely mortal beings, following their destiny. So it is among the staff of Camp Evergreen, an oasis of love in residential Sheboygan.

Camp Evergreen is a haven for youth and adults with cognitive challenges. Most require regular supervision, and their disabilities may keep them from assimilating into the general population. The outside world can be scary when you don't blend in. Camp Evergreen is the opposite, a comfortable blanket of familiarity among friends who are just like you.

The camp was founded in 1926 by Charles E. Broughton, whose hardscrabble upbringing made him a champion for the less fortunate. Born in 1873, his Wisconsin childhood was chockful of hard work. He husked corn, painted wagons, and helped the local blacksmith. At age 11, he left school for a job with a local newspaper. In his teens, he moved to

Sheboygan and worked for the *Sheboygan Press*, the town's flagship newspaper. He never left.

By middle age, the clean-shaven Broughton had become a *Sheboygan Press* icon. Each day, with cigar in mouth, he punched out influential editorials on a typewriter in his smoke-filled office. With his vest and loose tie, double chin, and round glasses, his appearance fit his profession.

Readers read his columns first. Everyone wanted to know what "Charlie" would opine about next. When he retired in 1952, Broughton was the newspaper's editor-in-chief and had won honorable mention for a Pulitzer Prize. It was a remarkable achievement for a man with only a fourth grade education.

Growing up poor, Broughton recalled long hours of arduous work. He missed out on the fun that comes with being a rough-and-tumble kid. So in 1926 at age 53, Broughton founded Kiddies Camp for underprivileged children. Here, in the summer, boys could enjoy regular meals, outdoor fun, make friends, and learn new skills—all things that the young Broughton never experienced. A single wooden building served as a dormitory and dining hall, set on several acres of land. Aft the camp's dedication ceremony, Broughton said, "You've got to do all you can to make your community a better place in which to live."[16]

Kiddies Camp was immensely popular. Donors, including Broughton, contributed money to keep camper fees low, and many of the staff volunteered. Broughton himself

---

[16] Today Sheboygan's Broughton Marsh Park is named in recognition of Broughton's efforts to restore the marsh, and Broughton Drive honors him for his community service.

The Quiet Icon

sometimes joined a game or ate a meal with the boys, finally enjoying the youth he never had.

The nonprofit camp was governed by a board of directors, including Bob's father. After Broughton's death in 1956, the directors, including Robert Sr., considered changing the camp's focus to serving people with cognitive challenges.

Chesebro told the directors, "Kiddies Camp is no longer unique. Other organizations are now serving 'poor kids,' such as the YMCA, Boys and Girls Clubs, and the Boy Scouts." He claimed that cognitively challenged kids now needed help. Who was doing that? These people were hidden from mainstream life. They deserved a place where they felt welcome, accepted, and could have fun without judgement.

Most directors nodded in agreement, and a motion to change the camp's mission passed. In 1980, the name Kiddies Camp was changed to Camp Evergreen.

In 2016, Bob was elected board president, and Paul Mason Jr., the camp director, retired. Mason was liked and admired. He'd earned a degree from Marquette University and was confined to a wheelchair due to cerebral palsy. Mason could relate to the disabilities of the camp's clientele.

Bob began networking for a leader. The top candidate was Mark Ellis, a middle-school teacher working with special-needs students. Ellis interviewed with Bob and Catherine Stayer, a prominent community volunteer.

Ellis arrived at Bob's home wearing a sport coat and tie. Bob and Catherine were casually dressed. They sat in the living room and Bob asked him questions. Why did he want the job? Could he raise funds? Why did he want to leave the school system? When could he begin work? Ellis answered patiently and thoughtfully, and Bob thought his demeanor was perfect for a challenging clientele.

Ellis was hired. The first priorities were to hire more staff and help raise funds for a new building. The original wood building, decayed and often leaking, was obsolete. Asking people for money was not something Ellis was used to doing. Bob told him not to worry, that he and Catherine Stayer would handle most of it. Bob and Wigwam Mills made the first substantial donations, and then Bob got to work. With the help of his brother-in-law Tom Roenitz, $600,000[17] was raised for the new facility, and Ellis never made a single fundraising call. The building was dedicated in 1990.

Ellis was happy with Evergreen's new home. It had most everything the camp needed: dormitory-style rooms, offices, a kitchen, and activity center. He said, "Bob was always asking for numbers, enrollment, where campers' families worked, and how can we make camp better and serve more people."

Today, the camp's mission reads:

> *To enrich the lives of children and adults with cognitive and other disabilities, as well as the lives of their families and care-providers, by offering accessible, compassion-driven, respite care, day services, after school care and summer camp programming.*

---

[17] About $1.5 million at the time of this book's publication.

The Quiet Icon

The traditional summer camp runs Monday through Friday with an impressive staff ratio of 3:1. Campers are ages 7 to 80. While some campers are relatively independent in their personal care, others require complete assistance with all of their day-to-day activities.

It's possible that Camp Evergreen's growth might have happened without Bob Chesebro, but his commitment made it a reality a lot sooner. Ellis remarked, "Bob was the driving force behind most everything you see here today. Hundreds of lives have been enhanced because of him, and personally, he changed my life."

* * *

In the shops and cafes of Elkhart Lake, Wisconsin, mentioning "Grasshopper Hill" shows that you just might be one of the locals. The words are sort of a password that identifies you as knowing the territory better than most.

Grasshopper Hill is not a secret. Basic research will uncover much information about this 25-acre nature preserve on the south shore of Elkhart Lake. But only the local residents seem to know about the hill and its history. They'll tell you that without Bob Chesebro, today's Grasshopper Hill and its preservation might never have been.

For generations, Grasshopper Hill was a landmark on the south shore of Elkhart Lake. It boasted beautiful vistas of the lake and surrounding agricultural and forested landscapes. Cows once grazed in the open pastures, and grasshoppers were thick in the summer. In his youth, Bob hiked to the top of the hill for picnic lunches and an occasional clandestine campfire. The property owners mostly ignored the trespassers, content to share their sanctuary with respectful visitors.

Around 2000, rumors began. The owners were going to sell Grasshopper Hill. The developers were circling, offering large sums of cash. Elkhart Lake's last bastion of wilderness shoreline was going to become scarred with roads and homes. There was even talk of a restaurant and a convenience store.

This was unacceptable. The keepers of Elkhart Lake gathered and decried that it couldn't be so. But it was true: Grasshopper Hill was for sale. There was a lot of handwringing and uneasiness until somebody suggested that this wasn't necessarily a bad thing. Maybe the new owner would keep the land undeveloped.

Somebody asked, "Why don't we buy it ourselves?" Another suggested contacting the Great Lakes Glacial Conservancy. Perhaps they would want to acquire Grasshopper Hill and preserve it.

A week later, representatives of the Conservancy visited the property. They saw mature trees, scenic vistas, grassy fields, and glacial geology. Everyone agreed that the property was worthy of preservation. But the purchase needed approval from the Glacial Lakes Conservancy board of directors, and even then, fundraising would be required. No money was available for an immediate acquisition.

The residents of Elkhart Lake crossed their fingers and waited for the Conservancy's decision. In 2006, the directors approved the purchase of Grasshopper Hill. The property owners agreed to a sale price, and fundraising began.

The Quiet Icon

Bob Chesebro supported the preservation of the hill. He said, "It is the right thing to do" and attended meetings about the hill's future. Once the Conservancy agreed to buy the land, he presented them with a $250,000 check. It happened quietly and without fanfare, but his longtime friend Bob Melzer defined the gift as monumental. "Bob essentially saved Grasshopper hill from the bulldozers," said Melzer. "Without Bob, the purchase might never have happened."

Bob's generosity created the Grasshopper Hill Preserve, a sanctuary for people who desire the tonic of nature. The Chesebro name isn't seen on signs, literature, or on the Conservancy's website, and that's just fine with Bob. "It's not about me," he said. "It's about helping others and making people happy."

* * *

Sheboygan's St. Clement Church impacted the Chesebro and Roenitz families as much as Wigwam Mills and the Roenitz Drug Stores. It was the source of their spiritual foundation, providing comfort and blessing in both good times and bad. It was the site of Bob and Katie's marriage and the baptism of their children. The Chesebro family worshiped there every Sunday. Bob sang in the choir, befriended the priests, and was a devoted parishioner.

Built in 1914, St. Clement Church in Sheboygan is named after the fourth bishop of Rome and a contemporary of the apostles. It was designed in the Low Gothic style with two square towers. Large, stained-glass windows bejewel each wall. It is a city landmark, steeped in tradition with a legacy of community service.

Bob supported St. Clement Church with personal financial donations, and asked others to contribute. As with most charities that he adopted, Bob delved into the operational details and discovered ways he could make things better.

His analysis revealed that more parishioners needed to give money. It's not that they weren't generous people; they just didn't understand how a nonprofit operates. Many assumed that money from the Sunday baskets was enough to pay for everything: the lights, heat, maintenance, landscaping, snow removal, and even the pastor's salary. Bob decided if they didn't understand the church's financial needs, he was going to educate them.

He assembled a series of parishioner listening sessions. First, Bob asked the attendees how the church could better meet their needs. Second, he explained why donating to the church was necessary. He made it simple. He showed a lengthy list of annual church expenses, then a short list of income. The two didn't balance, and there was a deficit. The only way to eliminate it was through donations.

This was a revelation to many, especially the Hispanic members, about 50 percent of the congregation. To them, "donating" meant cleaning for free, or providing a chicken dinner. After Bob's sessions, financial gifts to the church increased significantly. "He had a way of relating to people and that made him convincing," explained fellow parishioner Donna Wendlandt. Bob liked people, and people wanted to like him back. That usually meant trying to make Bob happy, even if it meant giving money.

Bob said, "Raising money for the parish was a gift of satisfaction. And I met many fine people."

Summarizing her father's charitable impact, Margaret stated, "My dad has touched so many lives. People in town tell me about what he's done and the impact he has made. Many people do things for recognition and accolades, but Dad never cared about that. He has always been humble."

Donna Wendlandt added, "Bob made Sheboygan a better place to live for many years to come. He's a true community steward."

ELKHART LAKE

Each year, thousands of tourists flock to Wisconsin. Cars from neighboring states are stuffed with happy faces, camping gear, and often are towing boats. On summer weekends, border traffic can seem to crawl.

Inspired, the Wisconsin Department of Tourism created a bumper sticker that read *Escape to Wisconsin*. The green and white sticker was seen everywhere, including remote regions of the world where Wisconsinites proudly left them behind.

Wisconsin is that kind of place. It may only take a few hours to get there, but across the border is a different world. The trees seem greener, the lakes are cleaner, and the sky is a deeper shade of blue. It's as if a passport was required for entry.

Wisconsin boasts remarkable geographic diversity. Three distinct regions have little in common except the state name. The north is a remote wilderness of forest, lakes, and rivers. The southwest is a mini mountain range of deep valleys, winding roads, trout streams, and charming villages. To the southeast, cows graze on expansive acres of grass, and fields of crops stretch for miles.

With so much variety, Wisconsinites may seldom vacation elsewhere. In just hours, a Badger State resident can seemingly be thousands of miles from home.

The Quiet Icon

So it is with Elkhart Lake, a half hour's drive west of Sheboygan. For decades, Elkhart Lake, and the nearby town of the same name, have enchanted generations of families. The statement "I'm going to Elkhart" is like saying "I'm escaping reality," and that life will magically improve upon crossing the city limits.

The American Indians claimed the lake had magic. The Potawatomi tribe traveled days to sit in the curative water. A visitor to Elkhart Lake in the late 1800s described the area:

> *We were never so favorably impressed with the beauty and loveliness of Lake Elkhart and its surroundings, and the advantages for enjoyment it offers the pleasure-seeker. Surrounded by innumerable hills which command beautiful prospects of the lake and vicinity, and numerous shady retreats where hours of enjoyment may be pleasantly passed, viewing the varied scenic splendor which greet the beholder on every side.*

Today, those restorative elixirs are also found in the town's restaurants, historic homes, parks, and resorts. An escape to Elkhart Lake assures a rejuvenated spirit, and leaving guarantees a sorrowful heart.

Elkhart Lake is the byproduct of well-off people who, for generations, have molded the area's character. Sheboygan Bay, on the lake's southwest shore, contains rows of historic homes and cottages that have never left family ownership. Names like Garton, Roenitz, Gunther, Vollrath, Bemis,

Elkhart Lake

Kohler, Liebl, Stayer, Reiss, and Prange are forever tied to the lake's legacy, sort of a Mt. Rushmore of historic area leaders.

Legacy families foster intense civic pride, with buildings and grounds groomed to strict codes. When a property is put up for sale, plans are quietly enacted to ensure that the new owners will meld into the Elkhart Lake culture. Outsiders can be viewed suspiciously until they demonstrate behavior the meets Elkhart Lake standards. Margaret recalled that "A California couple bought a home on the lake, and we joke that they became true locals after 20 years."

The Chesebro cottage rests atop a small hill overlooking the waters of Elkhart Lake. A windowed porch is the social center, boasting a long promenade of plush rattan and wood-framed furniture, rocking chairs, and comfortable sofas. Sheboygan Bay shines in the distance beyond a stand of stately cedar trees.

Behind the grand porch, window-paned doors invite guests to enter the dining room. An ample, painted wood table is surrounded by ten wooden chairs with caned seats. Windows allow diners to gaze at the north and east lake shorelines.

Upstairs, four bedrooms show the simple elegance of the 1930s, sporting classic iron bed frames and windows adorned with curtains and valances. The classic décor is completed by wooden chairs, mirrors, vanities, bedside lamps, and framed paintings hanging on wallpapered walls.

At the lakefront, sparkling-clear water beckons swimmers. The lake bottom, composed of sand and pea-

The Quiet Icon

The dining room of the Chesebro cottage on the shores of Elkhart Lake.

gravel, is knee-deep for about 20 yards before dropping off into darkness.

The cottage was purchased Bob's grandfather, H. Carl Prange. After H. Carl passed, Bob's mother and two of her siblings took ownership. When Bob and his brother were born in the late 1930s, their mother, Helen, became sole owner and custodian. The Chesebro Family lived there in summer, and Bob's father commuted to his Wigwam Mills office in Sheboygan.

In 1970, when Bob was 32 years old, he bought the Elkhart Lake cottage from his mother. After the sale, she warned him, "Nothing is worse than dual home ownership. Don't ever do something like that!"

Bob told her not to worry; he would not share the title to the family cottage. Then Bob's brother Jim phoned Bob from his home in Rochester, Minnesota. "Jim told me that he wanted to spend some time at Elkhart each summer and asked me to sell him a stake in the property. I remembered what my mother told me about shared ownership, so I told him 'no,' but said he could use the cottage for a month each year. I didn't want to sell any shares of it."

Jim said he'd consider it.

The matter seemed resolved until his mother intervened. "She told me that I needed to sell one-third of the property to Jim. She completely reversed her opinion about shared ownership." To this day, Dr. Jim Chesebro owns one-third of the Chesebro Family cottage.

Bob relocated his family to the Elkhart Lake every June and July, and he commuted 20 minutes each way to his Wigwam office. Like most everything he engaged with, the residents of Sheboygan Bay and Elkhart Lake quickly benefitted from Bob Chesebro's touch—most notably was the legend of "Big Blue."

For decades, "Big Blue" has been the centerpiece of Sheboygan Bay. In the spring, the large swimming raft is ceremoniously launched, signaling the start of summer. In fall, it's reluctantly pulled back to shore. In the early days, horses did that work. The raft is sort of seasonal timepiece, in addition to a water-based landmark. Today, about 30 families use it each summer.

Beth Guenther, Bob's cousin-once-removed, said, "Our family and Bob maintained 'Big Blue,' but Robert [Bob] is

The Quiet Icon

the primary caretaker and cheerleader. Over the years, he quietly financed the repairs and upgrades."

More than a raft, "Big Blue" also has a diving board and a water slide, making it sort of a mini-amusement park. It transformed Bob into a playful kid, characteristics that were usually masked by the responsibilities of running a large business.

Margaret remembered that "Dad would show us how to go down the slide on our backs, head first, into the water. One time, he said, 'I will give you a sock full of nickels if you can do a flip off of the diving board!'" That seemed scary, so even with the promised reward, neither Margaret nor Chris accepted the challenge. Finally, Bob said, "I'll show you how to do it." He walked confidently to the end of the diving board, took several deep breaths, bounced a few times, and then launched himself. Airborne, he rotated half-way and awkwardly flopped into the water. Surfacing, he had to admit to his children that "I am still working on it."

Over time, Bob and Big Blue became synonymous. He didn't own it, but he paid for upgrades and arranged the ceremonial spring launching. Sometimes he was seen vacuuming the raft's carpet.

One afternoon, Bob was alone on his raft. Youth from outside of Sheboygan Bay paddled over and climbed aboard. They shoved Bob into the lake and laughed, which prompted about a dozen shoreline residents to chase the perpetrators away. The push was an egregious breach of lake etiquette. Big Blue, and its king, had been violated. The stewards of Sheboygan Bay would have none of it.

Bob Chesebro, the "King of Big Blue," kneels in front of the iconic Elkhart Lake raft.

Besides the raft, Bob was passionate about sailing small boats. He was the first person on Elkhart Lake to own and use a windsurfer, and he could masterfully captain sailboats. "Dad loved to make the sailboat go really fast and tip it steeply," Margaret remembered. Friend John Rummele remarked that Bob "was an excellent sailor and waterskier. He could even do tricks."

The Chesebros never owned a large power boat. "That was just too flashy," said son Chris. "Mom and Dad preferred the silent paddle sports, such as a canoe or rowboat."

Chris explained, "I call Elkhart Lake the happiest place on earth. We lived there all summer, and would wake up and jump in water, ride our bikes, and swim all day until sunset."

Margaret said, "At Elkhart Lake, time stands still. As an adult, I took a Friday off work, went to the lake, and sat on the pier. After a while, I heard somebody walking on the pier, and it was Dad. He said to me, 'So, you're taking some time off, huh? Sometimes you need that. You have to take a break.'"

Bob had often done that himself. As the Potawatomi tribe discovered hundreds of years ago, Elkhart Lake renews the heart and soul.

THE HANDOFF

Both of Bob's children attended Villanova University, an Augustinian Catholic institution near Philadelphia. Margaret admitted that leaving home for college was tough. Her mother was undergoing cancer treatments, and going away felt like bad timing.

Before she left, Bob wrote her a letter:

Dear Margaret: August 20, 1996

This letter is somewhat of a combination of observations, suggestions, and feelings that I have about you starting your higher education.

First of all, I should say that your departing for Villanova is a matter of pride, happiness, and regret for me. I am proud of what you have accomplished thus far in your life, and the person that you have come to be. Your forthcoming absence will be difficult for me to adjust to, but nonetheless it will make my paternal heart grow fonder. Having said that, you know me well enough to know that I am more at ease conveying my feelings in this fashion, rather than blurting them out to you. I guess your mom is better at verbalizing these kinds of things.

The Quiet Icon

> *Please also understand that I realize you have feelings and convictions of what you are going to do. I went through the same process and experienced the challenges, the excitement, the initial feelings of slight trepidation and the adjustment of leaving home. At times you need to stretch to improve or get what you want. This requires that you take yourself out of your comfort zone at times.*

In August 1996, Bob flew with Margaret to Philadelphia and helped her move into her dormitory. Things got emotional and Margaret recalled, "When we parted ways, Dad was wearing dark sunglasses, but I could see tears coming from behind them. I'd never seen him cry before. I was crying too." Bob later admitted that it was one of the saddest days of his life.

Margaret got homesick. "Dad wrote me letters telling me about some of the struggles he had in college, and that helped", she remembered. "Sometimes you think that your parents are invincible, but Dad's letters humanized him and my homesickness."

Margaret graduated from Villanova with a degree in business administration and a concentration in marketing. She relocated to Minneapolis and took a marketing job with Gander Mountain, an outdoor recreational products store. Later, she worked for Fingerhut, an online retailer.

Two years later, Chris also graduated from Villanova with a major in business and minor in information technology. The business school curriculum seemed mundane, but he found the IT coursework fascinating. Topics like cybersecurity, hacking, database management, and coding weren't for everyone, but Chris naturally understood these complexities. He even decided that he "wanted to be a programmer and an IT guy." Computers were now integral to nearly everything, and programmers were in demand.

In 2000, after college, Chris moved to Boston and took a job in data base management with Cognos Inc., a business software company. Five years later, he signed on with the Bose Corporation. Both jobs required sophisticated and specialized work.

Chris liked the challenge of logic puzzles, particularly as they applied to people. He said, "If I can put people together in a way where it all works, that's a real logic puzzle accomplishment."

Chris met his future wife in Boston, Janine Elizabeth Rinke, who was also from Wisconsin. After their marriage in 2007, Chris enrolled in graduate school at Bentley University, located in Boston's Back Bay neighborhood. He graduated with distinction and accepted a master's degree in business administration.

Margaret and Chris were content in Minneapolis and Boston. They were energizing cities, a world apart from smaller Sheboygan. But even the big-city allures couldn't distract them from wondering if someday they might join the family business.

Margaret said "Dad would call me and say, 'Well, what do you think about coming back and doing this....'" Margaret would tell him no, she didn't want to do that. A few weeks later Bob would call again with another option.

Bob also called his son. "Dad kept calling me, asking if I was interested in a job with the company. Some of the offers were appealing, but the timing just didn't seem right."

In December 2006, Margaret was offered a job with Wigwam as field marketing manager. Bob told her that it was a newly created position, and that she could work remotely from Minneapolis. There was no need to move home. Her father had created a job that was tailored to her lifestyle, and Margaret accepted.

Three years later, in 2009, Margaret's phone rang. It was Jim Einhauser. He said, "Wigwam is looking for a director of sales for the Western portion of country. You'd be really good at that job." Margaret told him she wasn't qualified, but Einhauser disagreed, telling her that she had the knowledge, personality, and drive. He added, "Sometimes you have to challenge yourself. If it scares you, you probably need to do it."

After a visit to Sheboygan, Einhauser personally convinced her. Margaret took the job and began meeting with Wigwam sales reps on the West Coast, including Tom Nowhard from Lake Tahoe, California. They began a long-distance relationship and soon became engaged.

In 2013, Margaret was at another crossroads. Wigwam offered her the job of Director of Product Management, web and e-commerce. It was a promotion, but she would need to move to Sheboygan. Going home would be relatively easy, but her California fiancé might be reluctant. Leaving trendy and gorgeous Lake Tahoe, with dependable mild weather, would be a difficult sell.

The Handoff

Fiancé Tom agreed to join her in Wisconsin. They were married on June 29, 2013. Margaret reflected, "Dad never pushed me to come home. I made the decision on my own but could see glimmer in his eyes when I returned."

* * *

After accepting his graduate degree with distinction at Bentley University, Chris returned to Wisconsin and joined the family business. He recalled, "At one point, my dad said, 'you can sell it or you can try and run it.' I felt the latter was the right choice, so it made sense to come home."

He moved to Sheboygan in 2009 and began his Wigwam initiation. He spent a year working in each manufacturing department, observing everything he could. From knitting, finishing, the dye house, and the distribution center, every division required employees with specialized skills, and Chris needed to learn them. He didn't need to become a pro, but know just enough to understand how things worked.

This was remarkably similar to his father's first job with Wigwam in 1962, when the elder Chesebro told his son, Robert Jr, "Your job is simple. You're going to educate yourself about this business."

Soon Chris was appointed as Wigwam Manufacturing Process Manager, managing supply chain and yarn purchases, creating manufacturing efficiencies, and collaborating with the textile workers union. In 2012, he was promoted to Director of Operations.

* * *

Bob Chesebro knew something about business transitions.

In his youth, his father would talk about assuming the presidency of Wigwam from his own father, Herbert. Robert Sr. used words like "difficult" and "stressful," and then sipped a scotch and soda to soothe himself. To young Bob, they were just words with no impact on boyhood life.

In 1968, when his father finally handed him the president's gavel, Bob spoke similar adjectives. The changeover was demanding and at times, traumatic. His father was the face of Wigwam and the name Robert Chesebro Sr. was mentioned with all the other noteworthy local leaders—men like Kohler, Garton, Prange, and Reiss. This was lofty company, and thirty-year-old Bob wondered if he could live up to his father's legacy. He was different from his dad. His friends and mother assured him that he'd do just fine, but Bob endured many sleepless nights.

Nor did his father disappear. As chairman of the Wigwam board of directors, Bob's every move was assessed by his watchful dad.

Around 2016, amidst all of those memories, Bob contemplated stepping back and letting Margaret and Chris take over. The timing wasn't perfect. His children were still relatively new to Wigwam and needed more time and experience. It was clear that they had the "right stuff" to eventually assume leadership, but that was a few years down the road.

This was unknown territory. Historically, there was a seamless leadership transition from one Chesebro to the succeeding generation.

Now it was different. Under Bob's stewardship, Wigwam was as big as it had ever been. There was a

The Handoff

dynamic, national sales force and hundreds of employees. The marketplace had changed forever, altered by online shopping and multi-door retail stores. The production of Wigwam products was essentially the same, but selling them required new, creative approaches in the digital era.

Board member Richard Pauls remarked, "The changing marketplace was the most challenging time at Wigwam. The retail environment had transformed, and we needed to negotiate with the big players. There were many discussions about selling the company, but that was anathema to the Chesebro ethic. Bob was determined to keep the company local, and not sell out."

All of this contributed to Bob's desire to slow down. He was 78 years old, and his success had built a complex business that sometimes overwhelmed him.

Bob obsessed about managing this transition. He was up late at night, writing notes on his computer and thinking about what his father would have done. He prayed. He asked his closest friends for advice. As usual, Bob took ample time to think and contemplate. He hired a consultant to help guide him. Bob usually gave himself deadlines for decisions, but this was different. It was more than a business transaction; this was family.

He eventually decided on a somewhat revolutionary succession plan by appointing an interim president. This way, he could still be involved, but at a reduced level. The person would mentor Chris and Margaret, bridging the transition between the current and future Chesebro Family leadership.

The Quiet Icon

In 2014, a senior Wigwam staff member was named interim company president. He was a seasoned employee who began as a mechanic and worked his way up, becoming a supervisor, foreman, manager, and then head of plant operations. The new leader had a plethora of manufacturing knowledge and had mastered the Wigwam knitting process. Those skills served him well on the manufacturing floor, but in an executive office, managing multitudes of new obligations, was overpowering. Even with Bob's help, there was just too much to learn.

Bob began searching for a new leader. He hired a recruiting firm to find candidates. Bob pored over resumes and called those who had potential. Some were eliminated immediately. With just a phone call, Bob knew whether or not the person fit the company culture. Experience was important, but character and integrity were paramount.

The finalists were interviewed at the Wigwam Mills plant. Ultimately, an executive from a tailored-suit maker was hired. The new boss was a Chicago guy through and through, boasting an aggressive manner that was not the "Wisconsin way." In two years, he had alienated most of the staff, and over time, expanded the product line that resulted in company deficits.

Employee Jamie Rische said, "He was a very convincing person, but a fish out of water. He had a different mindset than the Chesebro mentality. It was his way, or no way." Several employees left the company during his leadership.

His smooth talking earned him three years at the helm before Bob and the board decided to part ways. Chris Chesebro remembered, "We tried to plan the transition smoothly, but it turned out messy." Margaret added, "The cultural fit was really hard for us. He wanted to run a family business more like a private equity firm. He had a different viewpoint on how you spend money and manage people."

On April 13, 2020, Chris and Margaret were named co-presidents. Even so, Chris said, "Margaret and I had to make a decision if we wanted to take over and run the company. Even after working there, we had to decide if we wanted to invest our lives in Wigwam."

In their hearts, it's likely that Chris and Margaret knew long ago that Wigwam was their mutual career destiny. The challenge was putting it into motion. Chris recalled, "It would have been difficult to just walk away from Wigwam. We wanted to be here for our family and the families of everyone who worked here. But we also recognized the burdens of carrying on a powerful legacy."

Two generations of Chesebro family leadership:
Robert E. Chesebro, Jr. (center) with
daughter Margaret (Chesebro) Newhard and son Chris Chesebro.

The Quiet Icon

Bob told his children, "Look, I have to step away now, and it is your business to run. For the sake of family dinners, I'm going to disengage."

Susan Kettler remembered, "When Margaret and Chris became co-presidents, it was reassuring because the family was back in control. It was a relief to everyone."

* * *

In the corporate universe, leadership transitions often bring change. New regimes look for ways to instill their culture and to make things better. Chris and Margaret looked over the Wigwam landscape and saw a stable company and a solid workforce.

The new leaders had proven themselves as competent businesspeople and were well-liked. Chris had a laid-back, easy demeanor with an infectious laugh. Margaret displayed a blend of grace and quiet strength. Their youthful charismas lifted spirits throughout the workforce. The general sentiment was that things at Wigwam were going to be good again.

The co-president duties were divided to accommodate Chris and Margaret's different skill sets. Margaret would manage marketing, sales, finance, and administration. Chris would oversee manufacturing, operations, and technology.

Chris stated, "My passion was always the people, not just the socks. We just hired two people, and they told me 'Wow, this is a really nice place to work.' I try to make sure that I embody my father's values of honesty and hard work, but I also want to be my own person. Nobody can be my dad."

The Handoff

The siblings listed their corporate priorities. First was addressing the Wigwam Mills factory. The large building was necessary when business was robust. By 2020, a shrinking market share and reduced production made the overhead costs unsustainable.

The plant was put up for sale and bought by Johnsonville, Inc.,[18] a local sausage manufacturer with a worldwide customer base. Margaret said, "At that point in our history, it made financial sense to rent. The old facility was just too large."

A vacant building was leased along Highway 42, just northwest of Sheboygan. The footprint was about 70 percent smaller than the former plant. Moving began in December 2020 and was finished in early January 2021, with only a few weeks of downtime.

Chris noted, "Moving into the new facility was a blessing. It gave Margaret and me a fresh start, without any ties to the past."

Jamie Rische added, "Moving to a new location was the best thing the company ever did. When we right-sized, we went back to our roots. Everything was more personal again, and employee interactions really improved."

---

[18] Johnsonville has its own, unique local story. It was founded in 1945 by Alice and Ralph F. Stayer as a butcher shop. They named it Johnsonville, after their Wisconsin hometown.

EVERYWHERE AND ANYWHERE

Wigwam socks are shipped to all 50 states and many countries across the globe. They arrive at large warehouses or at the small-town post office used by cobblers, saddleries, or tack shops. Some are delivered to general stores, built a century ago and still operated by the same family.

Over the years, the small "mom and pop" shops have been the lifeblood of Wigwam sales. The owners never thought they'd start an outdoor retail store. That was for other people. They were too busy fishing, running, biking, or skiing.

Many of these shops have remarkable histories. Like Wigwam, they began as small family businesses and grew based on their reputation for quality products, and exceptional customer service.

Angerman's

Angerman's is located in Wrangell, Alaska, on a small island off the southern coast. Wrangell has a population of around 2,000 people, and Angerman's has sold Wigwam products dating to the early 1970s. There is no road access, so shipments arrive by boat or by air. For years, the Angermans placed their orders by letter, mailed to the Wigwam office in Wisconsin. The request was handwritten on vintage letterhead, with the store name and address embossed on the top of the paper.[19]

Cabela's

Cabela's was started in 1960 by brothers Dick and Jim Cabela, who sold and shipped fishing lures to mail-order customers. Later, they opened a hunting and fishing shop in remote Sidney, Nebraska, population 6,000. Sidney is a three-hour drive from Denver International Airport. For years, there was just one motel in town.

Eventually, the business grew into a juggernaut and was purchased by Bass Pro Shops.

DICK'S Sporting Goods

In 1948, 18-year-old Dick Stack borrowed $300 from his grandmother's cookie jar. An avid fisherman, Dick founded DICK'S Sporting Goods that same year. By the 1960s, DICK'S was a complete sporting goods shop and sold Wigwam socks and hats. Ed Stack, Dick's son, became the CEO, but Bob remembers when he was the Wigwam sock buyer. DICK's Sporting Goods is now one of the largest sporting goods retailers in the nation with more than 800 locations.

---

[19] Angerman's remains in business as of this publication date. The tag line on their Facebook page reads, "Name-brand family clothing, footwear, workwear, hunting and fishing gear, licenses, Alaska souvenirs, gifts, jewelry and much more!"

Frank's Sport Shop

Frank's Sport Shop opened in the Bronx in 1921, and has supplied Wigwam socks to its customers since 1958. It's located in a rough part of town, but that doesn't deter customers or Wigwam sales representatives. One salesman's car was repeatedly broken into and his samples stolen. He continued to service the store and hired a security man to watch his vehicle. Bob admitted, "You didn't go to Frank's unless you had some assurance you would be safe. But they have great loyalty to our brand."

Honus Wagner Sporting Goods

Honus Wagner is often said to be the greatest baseball star ever to take the diamond.

From 1897 to 1917, Wagner played shortstop for 21 seasons in Major League Baseball, almost entirely for the Pittsburgh Pirates. He won eight batting titles, a record that remains unbroken. He led the league in slugging six times, and stolen bases five times. In 1936, the Baseball Hall of Fame inducted Wagner as one of its first five members, along with Ty Cobb and Babe Ruth. An early Wagner baseball card is considered one of the most valuable in existence.

After his retirement from the big leagues in 1919, Honus opened a sporting goods store bearing his name in downtown Pittsburgh. Nobody is certain if Wigwam socks were sold directly to Honus Wagner, but for decades,

Wigwam products were sold at Honus Wagner Sporting Goods.[20] During the school year, coaches at the Pittsburgh high schools instructed there athletes to head to Honus Sporting Goods and buy two pairs of Wigwam athletic socks. The coaches said, "Nothing is better to keep your feet comfortable and protected from blisters."

McGuckin Hardware

McGuckin Hardware opened in Boulder, Colorado, when it was a small western town. Besides the University of Colorado, there were few reasons to go there. Ski meccas like Aspen and Vail were still wilderness, and mountain roads were narrow and primitive.

For a long time, McGuckin Hardware was the only general store in Boulder. It had four employees, and its shelves were stuffed with merchandise, including Wigwam socks and hats. The aisles were so narrow that customers rubbed shoulders. Founder Bill McGuckin was an avid fly fisherman who wore Wigwam socks to keep his feet warm in the cold rivers. He claimed there was no better sock to keep your feet toasty, even in freezing water.

Today, McGuckin has more than 250 employees and boasts a store the size of a football field. It's so cavernous that it's not unusual for customers to get lost. Wigwam socks were on McGuckin shelves from the beginning and remain there today.

---

[20] The sole Honus Wagner Sporting Goods store closed in 2011.

Everywhere and Anywhere

The National Football League (NFL)
The Green Bay Packers players' use Wigwam socks at practice and the kickers wear them on game days. The New Orleans Saints, Minnesota Vikings, and the Arizona Cardinals have been known to wear Wigwam socks, hats, and gloves.

Tom Barnes, an NFL referee, was a Wigwam sales representative for nearly 40 years. When he retired from the NFL in 2012, he was the longest standing referee in the league. In all, Barnes worked 513 total games including 17 playoff games, three Pro Bowls, six conference championships, and Super Bowl XXVIII (28) in 1994.

Nordstrom
Nordstrom began as a family-owned shoe store in 1901. Decades later, it became a leader in fashion apparel. Every store has something in common: No matter what door you enter, you will be in the shoe department, and that feature remains today.

Paragon Sporting Goods
Paragon Sporting Goods was founded in 1908 in New York City, at 18th Street and Broadway. It remains owned by the same family, but the store now encompasses several adjacent buildings and six floors. Wigwam socks have been sold on almost every floor, and even in the basement.

For first-time visitors, navigating the aisles of Paragon can be overwhelming. Nooks and crannies unlock sporting discoveries around every corner. Customers can find equipment for every sporting activity, from the finest baseball mitts to exclusive rods for fly-fishing. There are even items for Bossaball, Hornussen, and Jai-Alai. Paragon opened the first ski store in New York City. Owner Sid Blank organized bus trips to Hunter Mountain, about four hours away. When the skiers returned around midnight, Sid opened the store so they could shop. Many skiers bought Wigwam socks and some even wore them home. Bob said, "Paragon is one of our key accounts in New York City."

REI (Recreational Equipment, Inc.)

REI began in 1935 when Seattle-based outdoorspeople Mary and Lloyd Anderson made a conscious decision: they needed a better way to purchase ice axes and climbing gear.

At the time, quality ice axes were available locally for $20, a hefty sum back then. To get better prices, Lloyd began ordering quality ice axes directly from Austria, relying on Mary's German skills to translate the catalogs. This way, they could get beautiful Austrian ice axes delivered to Seattle at the mere cost of $3.50, including postage.

Friends and colleagues learned of their strategy and wanted to buy in. Lloyd and Mary decided to collect their money, which would increase buying power and lower the cost of goods for all. The co-op was born and Wigwam products were sold in REI's first shop.

Today, REI is an outdoor mecca co-op of hundreds of stores, along with a catalog and on-line business. Jim Whittaker, who summited Mt. Everest in the 1950s, became REI's president in the 1960s. Jim was an advocate for Wigwam socks, and Wigwam supplied his family's climbing school on Mt. Rainer. Wigwam socks have been worn on many summits of Mt. Everest and other high peaks around the globe.

SAM's Outdoor Outfitters

SAM's Outdoor Outfitters (Sam's Department Store) started in 1932 as an army and navy surplus store in Brattleboro, Vermont. It's a family-owned, third-generation business. Three generations of the Barofsky family have sold Wigwam products and have also provided Wigwam sales reps with tremendous customer insights.

Schroeder Bros. Department Store and Evanoff's

Schroeder Bros. Department Store is located in Two Rivers, Wisconsin, population 11,270. Founded in 1891, its two-story brick building offers a bustling marketplace and a glimpse into the glory days of the big department stores, such as Higby's in the Christmas movie classic, "A Christmas Story." Wigwam products have been on the shelves of Schroeder's since 1940. Like Wigwam, the Schroeder Family generously supports their community.

Another small town, Sheboygan Falls, is just ten minutes away from the Wigwam plant. Bob's father began selling to Evanoff's in 1954. Evanoff's sells nearly everything for daily living, and the family still picks up their sock orders right at the Wigwam facility. Shopping at Evanoff's is an old-time, Main Street experience. Bob said, "Evanoff's loves Wigwam, and they have been a classic account for decades."

The Quiet Icon

The U.S. Military
Wigwam products are worn by American soldiers across the globe. Wigwam supplies the Naval Academy, the Air Force, the Army, and the Marine Corps.

Charities
In 1909, the Milton Hershey School was started by chocolate magnate Milton S. Hershey and his wife, Catherine. The Hersheys were unable to have their own children, so they used their blessings to create a boarding school for orphaned kids. Today, the Milton Hersey School provides cost-free, private, co-educational school for children of low-income families with the goal of preparing them for a productive life. Wigwam is the school's sole supplier of socks.

Lighthouse Mission in Bellingham, Washington provides the homeless with shelter, food, clothing, and guidance. Wigwam has donated thousands of pairs of socks and warm-weather clothing to Lighthouse Mission.

The Story of Costco and Wigwam
In the early 2000s, Costco was selling Wigwam socks without Bob's knowledge. He checked with his sales representatives. Nobody had Costco as a client, but some claimed that Wigwam inventory was indeed on Costco shelves.

Bob investigated. The culprit was a southern California retailer that was diverting large quantities of their Wigwam inventory to Costco, a scheme employed by unscrupulous retailers to make a profit. Bob stopped selling to the perpetrator, effectively ending the diversion of Wigwam merchandise to Costco.

Costco noticed. They called and asked if Wigwam would sell directly to them. Bob said "no," but the company would consider making a private label for them under their Kirkland brand. A meeting was arranged at the Costco offices in Issaquah, Washington.

Bruce Gordon, the Director of Wigwam Sales at the time, and Jim Einhauser arrived in Issaquah. Einhauser said, "It was very unusual for Costco's upper management to attend a product presentation. Usually they distance themselves from the suppliers."

Gordon and Einhauser entered the meeting room. Greetings were exchanged, and a Costco executive asked if they would sell the Wigwam brand to them. Einhauser told them "no" but suggested an alternative. The Costco executives pivoted and walked out the door. The meeting lasted 45 seconds.

Years later, Costco became one of the best retailers in the country. Their formula allows them to sell premium products at great prices. Their Kirkland brand is top quality, so Bob decided to have another try with Costco and succeeded. They agreed to sell three-packs of Wigwam's popular Moraine sock, and sales for both Costco and Wigwam were robust.

The partnership lasted 12 years. Like all of Costco's suppliers, Wigwam underwent Costco's stringent annual review process. Their quality-control people travel globally visiting suppliers to test and verify merchandise. Each Wigwam product was compared to the competition, including its quality, value, and even packaging. The manufacturing facilities were also examined. Wigwam always passed.

The Quiet Icon

In July 2015, Jim Einhauser's phone rang. It was the interim president of Wigwam. He told Einhauser that Costco had rejected the year's entire order, claiming yarn was not as specified.

Although he was retired, Einhauser offered to drive to Costco's main office. The Costco team liked Einhauser, so he hoped for a fast resolution. The interim president told him "no," it was too late. So Einhauser checked with Bob, who told him not to bother. Costco was holding firm.

One account never defined the Wigwam brand. There are countless success stories and hundreds of great relationships forged during Wigwam's long existence as an American-made, iconic brand.

ATTITUDE AND INSPIRATION

Bob's family knew something was wrong because he stayed home most days. His hands shook, making simple activities such as using utensils, holding a glass, and writing a challenge.

Katie and Margaret drove him to the Mayo Clinic in Minnesota, where he was initially diagnosed with essential tremor, a motor disease, and later, supranuclear palsy, similar to Parkinson's disease. They planted a device in Bob's brain that delivers electrical impulses that interrupt the signals that cause tremor muscle movements.

The device seemed to help, but other symptoms surfaced, including imbalance and speech complications. Margaret said, "It was challenging for him, though he would never let on to that. He worked tirelessly to find a diagnosis and has continued to push for conclusions and associated treatments." Bob went to both physical and speech therapies and underwent neurological chiropractic treatment.

With these afflictions, many people become sedentary. Bob was resolute to stay in shape, and he regularly went to the Sheboygan YMCA. According to Donna Wendlant, "When I see him come into the Y with his cane to work out, it makes me feel guilty that I haven't worked out. Bob never viewed himself as a victim."

Margaret admires that her father "led by example through dealing with the changes in his life. He has focused on the things in his life that drive him and make him happy (beyond Wigwam), such as his children and the need for individual gratitude."

Bob's positive demeanor was supercharged by watching Katie confront her own health problems. In 1996, she was diagnosed with multiple myeloma, a cancer of the bone marrow that compromises the immune system. The cancerous cells multiply rapidly, crowding out healthy cells within the bone marrow. The disease is rare, affecting only about 100,000 people in the United States. Although it's not hereditary, Katie's sister Jo Ellen succumbed to it, and sister Chris is presently stricken.

Multiple myeloma is sneaky and suspicious. Like most cancers, there is no cure, and treatments are often experimental. Katie underwent two stem cell transplants, chemotherapy, and numerous clinical studies and drug trials.

At one point, Bob moved to Rochester and supported her through treatments and recovery. Margaret said, "If ever there was an indicator of the strength of their marriage and devotion, that was it." She added, "There were three instances when we were convinced Mom would meet God. One of them was when I asked her at the hospital, *Do you know who I am?* She nodded, but when I asked her to identify me, she couldn't say. I replied, *It's okay, I know that you know me.*

Attitude and Inspiration

Before she left for college, Bob wrote to his daughter:

Needless to say, Mom's illness is difficult for you, Chris, and I to bear as it is for her. Rest assured that I am and will try to do everything possible to make her more comfortable and to be certain that she gets the best attention and care. Although there are no guarantees, both Mom and I are in a fighting and determined mood and are going to do our level best to fight her condition and overcome it. As tough as it has been for her, she has certainly summoned her faith in God, positive attitude, and determination to overcome her condition. Even the doctors have told us this is important, although they can't measure the impact of it. It is certainly possible for her to recover, and we are both working toward that goal.

True to her character, Katie outsmarted another life impediment. She lived longer than most multiple myeloma patients, nearly 27 years. The constant treatments affected her body, but she still gardened and played golf. Katie passed on February 18, 2025.

Katie's sister Chris explained, "There is no 'woe is me' in my family. All of the Roenitz siblings had medical issues, and we just deal with it."

Dealing with life is a natural human condition. In the end, what happens to you is less important than how you respond to it. Attitude, honesty, and humility matter. It's the Bob Chesebro way of doing things.

Above all else, that is why Bob Chesebro leaves a legacy of people who love him.

ACKNOWLEDGEMENTS

For this book, Bob Chesebro asked me to interview thirty people. During those conversations, I learned that everyone keeps Bob, Wigwam Mills, or both, in their life for eternity. The reasons range from sheer love for the man, to steadfast devotion to a company that gave them a chance.

Writing a biography is not something that you can do alone. It requires hours of insights and recollections from people who have their own, busy lives. I'm grateful that all of them allowed me to poke around and ask questions about a man in his eighth decade of life and a fourth-generation company. There was a lot to learn.

Everyone I spoke with used similar adjectives. Bob Chesebro is kind, hardworking, funny, giving, devoted, and just an all-around good guy. At times, I hoped that somebody might tell an unknown, clandestine story. An episode of decadence, for example, can add a lot of spice to a book.

That never happened. Although nobody said it this way, it was clear that Robert E. Chesebro is a saintly man who has always done the right thing.

I am particularly grateful to Jon Doll, a friend since childhood. Jon introduced me to Bob, and this book may not have happened without Jon's endorsement and enthusiasm.

The Quiet Icon

The Doll family has their own Sheboygan legacy, and Jon's and my parents were best friends through life.

My appreciation also extends to the following people for sharing their time and memories with me:

Katie and Robert E. Chesebro
Christopher Chesebro
Jim Einhauser
Mark Ellis
Dave Fischer
Beth Gunther
Peter Gunther
Fred Heider
Cristal Hodges
Eleanor "Tippy" Jung
Susan Kettler
Lollie Prange Krawitt
Bob Melzer
Don Meszaros
Margaret Newhard
Richard Pauls
Hal Peters
Russ Pilling
Jamie Rische
Chris Roenitz
Robert Roenitz
John Rummle
Donna Wendlandt
John Wilder

Chapter Title

Thanks to the Elkhart Lake Historical Society and Ariana Melzer, whose coffee-table book about Wigwam's first hundred years was eminently helpful. Jim Einhauser submitted pages of behind-the-scenes memories and insights.

Finally, I am grateful to Robert E. Chesebro Jr. for entrusting me to write his biography. It was a rewarding journey.

About the Author

Jon Helminiak is a native of Wisconsin. He currently divides his time between Land O' Lakes, Wisconsin, and Oro Valley, Arizona.

His other books include:

Nothing Routine – *A Quest for Adventure in Remote and Strange Places*
Inverted Climb – *The Remarkable Life of Terry J. Kohler*
UNLIMITED – *An American Fighter Pilot's Gamble with Life*
This Token of Freedom – *A Remarkable Wartime Journey*
Land O' Lakes – *The History*
Course Set for Manito-wish
Walk East in the Morning: *The Newspaper and Magazine Articles of Raymond Helminiak*
Influence – *The Wisdom of Elmer F. Ott*

www.ingramcontent.com/pod-product-compliance
Lightning Source LLC
Chambersburg PA
CBHW050030090426
42735CB00021B/3430